Lords of the Links

The Story of Professional Golf

Geoffrey Cousins

Hutchinson Benham, London

335218
796-352

Hutchinson Benham Limited
3 Fitzroy Square, London W1

An imprint of the Hutchinson Group

London Melbourne Sydney Auckland
Wellington Johannesburg and agencies
throughout the world

First published 1977
© Geoffrey Cousins, 1977

Set in Monotype Baskerville

Printed in Great Britain by
Ebenezer Baylis and Son Ltd,
The Trinity Press, Worcester, and London,
and bound by Wm Brendon & Son Ltd,
Tiptree, Essex

ISBN 0 09 131560 3

Contents

List of Illustrations

The Honor Award of the USPGA

'Mine age is even as nothing.' James Sherlock and
  George Duncan competing in the Teacher Senior
  Championship at Fulwell in 1957

Between pages 136 and 137

The stampede to the home green as the 1957 Ryder Cup
  match drew to a close at Lindrick

Moment of triumph. Dai Rees with the Ryder Cup
  chaired by his team at Lindrick

Tony Jacklin with the Open Championship Cup at
  Lytham in 1969

'The Commander' and friends. Charles Roe, with George
  Gibson and Lord Brabazon of Tara, at his retirement
  dinner in 1961

Lord Derby, President of the PGA, lays the cornerstone
  of the new headquarters at The Belfry, Sutton
  Coldfield

Artist's impression of The Belfry, showing the new PGA
  headquarters

Head office and regional secretariat assembled at the
  opening of the new headquarters

The Tournament Players' Division team

Introduction

This history covering one and a half centuries has as centrepiece the events of the past seventy-five years – the life span so far of The Professional Golfers' Association of Great Britain and Ireland during which the prizemoney tournament programme grew from almost nothing to its present worldwide expanse. Some of this material appeared in serial form in the Association's Journal, but has been extensively revised, with additional chapters recording the important happenings of the past three years.

My extensive research has had valuable assistance from many sources, not least the records kept by the late Commander R. C. T. Roe during his twenty-eight years as Secretary. From the present secretary Colin Snape and from Donald Case and other members of the headquarters staff I have had all possible help. I am specially indebted to Leslie J. Taylor, son of J. H. Taylor, who traced for me the activities of his father in starting the movement leading to the foundation of the PGA.

George Gibson, one-time managing director of the Professional Golfers' Co-operative Association, and the present chief, Marshall Lumsden, have both provided useful information on the business side, and in addition I have been allowed to browse through the extensive library collected by Mr Gibson and housed in the PGCA offices at Putney.

1*

Many golfers and relatives of golfers have been of great assistance in providing information, reminiscences and photographs, and particular thanks are due to H. le Fleming Shepherd of Stanmore; the Revd T. W. Richardson, M.A., Secretary of Notts Golf Club; Mrs Nancy Box of Wrotham Heath, Sevenoaks; G. W. D. Baker of Littlestone, Kent; Donald Ellis of Plymouth; Mrs Mary Rowlands of Chalfont St Peter; P. Laidlaw of Temple, Midlothian; Ernest Preston of Northwood, Middlesex; Mrs Phyllis Pugsley of Bridgwater, Somerset; Sidney Doctors of Brighton; J. Steer of Huddersfield; and Ray Whiting of Allingham, Lincs.

Prologue

The scene has all the elements of a jousting-field in front of a medieval castle. The clubhouse forms the backcloth for a home green flanked by lofty stands packed with fair ladies and bronzed gentlemen applauding each pair of entrants to the lists. There are no farthingales or wimples, no doublets or hosen, no gleaming armour or threatening lances, no giant destriers pawing the ground with iron-shod hooves. But there is no doubt about the excitement. Some of the spectators have been in those stands all day watching the last approaches and putts and scanning the scoreboard to keep in touch with progress on the course. Most have spent the day following the chief contestants from one vantage point to another. But now the day approaches its climax and every seat is occupied. The competitors arrive two by two to make their final thrusts, greeted by applause varying in volume according to their positions or reputations, but never less than warm. No matter how hopeless the individual's position he has played his part for four days and even now can make a dramatic gesture, a deadly bunker shot or a long putt holed, before leaving the stage.

As the couples appear in turn then disappear into the wings the excitement grows, in expectation of the last act in the tussle between the two leaders who even now can be seen walking from the seventeenth green to the eighteenth teeing-ground – a young but tough home golfer and a tall, experienced player from overseas. The news arrives that the youngster still holds a lead of one stroke and a hush descends on the crowded stands and the larger crowds lining both sides of the fairway. The leader stands to his ball with apparent unconcern and the full vigorous swing which has carried him so far does not fail in this final test. The ball flies straight and far, pitches on the centre of the fairway and comes to rest, ideally placed for the shot to the green. The older man, rich in experience and wise in golfing ways, makes an equally good drive and they walk on, followed by a mass of onlookers who so far have been restricted by fences but can now fall in behind, ready to rush ahead when the second shots have been played, to close the open end of the jousting-field.

The pressure is on for everyone; for the tense spectators, for the youngster on the brink of success, for the seasoned player who has been through it all before. Everything depends on the next two or three strokes and there is complete silence as the old campaigner, with no sign of nerves, sends his ball flying straight to the green, to pitch short and run to within five yards of the pin. For the younger man this is the moment of greatest tension. The least relaxation of concentration, the slightest error in the swing, even a microscopic divergence from the proper contact point on the club-face, could be ruinous. All hangs on what happens in the next few seconds, and in such situations players are asked for what, in most cases, is beyond their powers. But this young man is one of the exceptions. Undisturbed by, perhaps scarcely aware of, the spectators massed behind him and the crowded stands ahead, he takes the chosen club, settles down for the shot and lets fly. The ball is scarcely airborne before the cheers start, to grow in volume and erupt in terrific applause as the ball rolls to a stop. The youngster is 'inside' his rival, by not much more than a yard, but near enough to the hole to give reasonable certainty of getting down in two putts for a par four. Thousands of people have seen the result of that stroke but not the man who made it. Overwhelmed by a flood of running spectators as soon as the ball left the clubhead, he at length emerges from the mob followed by his caddie, and walks on to the green to a crescendo of applause. He throws up his arms in an involuntary gesture of delight. He is the conquering hero but, being a boy at heart, is savouring not the satisfaction of conquest but merely the joy of achievement.

This is the moment, the climax of years of apprentice-ship and painful groping towards proficiency, months of consolidation in the front rank, and weeks of prepara-tion towards such a goal as now opens before him. The hush following the cheering, as the men prepare to putt, is almost spine-chilling in its contrast. There is still so much in suspense. The euphoria among the young man's supporters engendered by that magnificent approach shot gives way to nail-biting anxiety as the chances are assessed. The experienced golfer from far-off parts is one of the world's best putters and five yards is no distance for him. If he holes and the lad takes three putts! There is dead silence as the ball begins its journey. It's on the right line and has the right strength but in the last few inches it fades away, to rest on the very lip of the hole. Now it is the youngster's turn and he faces the supreme test, for pressure suddenly relieved can be dangerous. So easy, with two for the championship, to be over-confident or over-cautious. Our young man is neither. With nerveless fingers he putts firmly and the ball runs to within six inches of the hole. A moment later it is tapped in, and the cheers from the stands, the crowds on the fairway and the watchers in the clubhouse split the skies. The new champion throws his ball into the crowd, raises arms and putter to acknowledge the salute, and turns to shake hands with his defeated rival and the two caddies. The fair ladies flutter their hands at the victorious knight and the bronzed gentlemen shout themselves hoarse. The tourney is over and the champion is carried away to receive his crown of laurels.

He receives also a cheque for more money than he has won in the previous twelve months, and the exclusive attention of the media. In the interview room he submits to questions designed to probe his inmost thoughts, his impressions before, during and after the contest, his past hopes, present feelings and future intentions. He sits under the bright lights with clicking cameras around him, outwardly composed but inwardly in a turmoil. He has been in such a seat before, as winner of an ordinary tournament, but now he is champion, and the difference is pleasantly alarming. He is suffering from the reaction, of course, but soon will be himself again and assured of a rosy future, for a modern golf champion will not be forgotten by the public until he has profited handsomely from his triumph. During the next few days his manager will set up dozens of rewarding projects and offers. There will be contracts to sign, programmes to arrange. Life will be different, harder, but enjoyable all the same. The winner can bask for a while in the general adulation, but basking time will soon be over and the call will come to work even harder than before.

There is much labour, much need of physical fitness and mental alertness, much reliance on sound psychology, in the daily life of a star golfer. But the rewards are well worth while even at a modest level of achievement, and the best players can soon amass fortunes. The cheques come not only from the hands of tournament sponsors. They come also from newspapers, publishers, makers of commodities – some far removed from the context of golf – and from overseas promoters calling the stars to all parts of the world. There is no business like the golf business, and the men who get most out of it are those who, few in comparison with the hordes of hopefuls, have made the grade and can travel the world, giving constant entertainment and picking up the prizes. They are the twentieth-century equivalent of the knights of the jousting-ring. They are the darlings of the galleries, the commanders of adoring armies. They are the lords of the links.

CHAPTER ONE
Toilers on the links

They were not always lords. For many years they were
merely the servants of lairds, toilers in the lower strata
of Scottish feudal society, having neither position nor
privileges, subject to the whims and fancies of their
casual employers and victims of an unsettled existence
on usually meagre earnings. They were engaged in a
variety of occupations on and around the links. They
made clubs and balls, carried clubs for hire, sometimes
coached or played with amateurs, and in between were
general hangers-on, part of the golfing scene but never
with more than walking-on roles. The ablest players
among them were engaged as partners for amateurs in
ordinary matches, and competed among themselves
for stakes usually put up by their backers. There was
no question, 150 years ago, of their being described as
professionals. The golfing vocabulary contained no
such word, and for much the same reason no one called
the gentleman golfer 'amateur'. The forerunners of
the present-day professionals were artisans, members
of the working class. The amateur, as he was to be
called later, was of the upper classes or the aristocracy.
And the fence between was insurmountable.

This situation had endured for at least a couple of
centuries when Queen Victoria came to the throne.
Although golf had been a popular pastime in Scotland
for a long but uncharted period, certainly since the

fifteenth century, only the upper classes had the time and money to play in a sophisticated way with the best and therefore most expensive equipment. Clubs ranged in quality from rough sticks cut from the hedgerows to properly-designed instruments fashioned by craftsmen who turned their skills to that particular end. Their transition from other operations to clubmaking was exemplified by the case of William Mayne, appointed clubmaker to James I in 1603, for he was a maker of bows and spears for the King's forces. The same monarch in 1618 granted a ball-making monopoly to James Melville, another Scot who for nearly thirty years had the sole right, through agents and assistants, of making and selling the feather-stuffed balls then in use.

The heads of wooden clubs were made from hard woods, a favourite being blackthorn, cut from the hedges in such a way that the natural bend where the stem grew from the main branch could form the neck and provide a means for fixing the shaft, usually of ash, to the head. This was done in several ways but in most cases by bevelling the shaft longitudinally, doing the same with the neck of the head, glueing them together and binding with twine. It may be imagined that the process produced widely different results according to the materials used and the skill of the worker, and craftsmen like Mayne – accustomed to fashioning bows, which had to provide strength with spring, and spears, which had to be carefully balanced – were adept at constructing golf clubs which came 'easy to the hand'. Naturally the best clubs commanded the highest prices, and those who followed Mayne and the other craftsmen of Stuart times continually improved the design and manufacturing techniques.

The golf ball itself passed through no such gradual transition during the same period of two or three hundred years, apart from changes in the quality of materials and no doubt some labour-saving devices to ease the laborious manufacturing process. Essentially it consisted of a leather case packed with feathers, and in that form existed from before Melville's time to the middle of the nineteenth century, when it was made a museum piece almost overnight by the introduction of the gutta-percha solid ball. The feather-ball maker cut segments of cowhide which, when stitched together and turned inside out, formed a roughly spherical bag. One joint was left partly open and through that hole the workman stuffed feathers until it was full almost to bursting-point. The feathers were boiled to make them manageable, but the labour of stuffing, particularly in the closing stages when the workman used a wooden ram fixed to a plate pressing on his chest, was exhausting and dangerous to the health. With the small hole closed and the ball hammered into a reasonable spherical shape, it was painted white to show up in the gorse, heather and rough grass covering the links. So long and hard was the process that the best makers could not produce more than three or four balls in a day, so they sold at prices beyond the reach of most artisans.

Those engaged in making clubs and balls were of course artisans, and some were very good players. But there were others of the working class also skilled at golf, including John Patersone, a cobbler who partnered the Duke of York, later James II, in a match at Leith against two English noblemen. His contribution to the success of his side was so effective that the Duke presented him with half the stake won, a large enough sum to enable him to build a house in Edinburgh and achieve a position which years of cobbling would not have provided. It was an early example of golfing prowess being rewarded handsomely, and no doubt the Duke's gift aroused as much envy among the other golfing artisans as that felt by unsuccessful players when large cheques are handed to the stars of today. But the Patersone incident was an exception then, for those who made their living at trades or at golf endured hard and uncertain work and enjoyed but modest remuneration.

During Stuart times the links of Leith and St Andrews were the chief golfing centres and the greatest activity was at Leith, from its proximity to Edinburgh, the seat of government in Scotland. Leith links was also the resort of those notabilities of the capital who, in 1744, started the first golf competition, made the first rules of golf, and formed the informal society which became the Honourable Company of Edinburgh Golfers, established for many years now at Muirfield, near North Berwick. Many of those Edinburgh gentlemen-golfers also played at St Andrews and, with the local lairds and gentry, formed a society there in 1754 which became the Royal and Ancient Golf Club, now the ruling body of the game. Although golf was also being played at Perth, Carnoustie, Montrose and other places in the East of Scotland, Edinburgh the government seat and St Andrews the ancient university city were the principal focal points for players of the upper classes, although since all the links were public places and anyone could play on them without charge the lairds and gentlemen enjoyed no priority beyond that accorded them by traditional respect. Nevertheless they had the twin advantages of time and money. At Leith, Musselburgh and Bruntsfield in the Edinburgh district and on the famous links of St Andrews they exercised themselves with the ease and *bonhomie* of men who had both leisure and cash to spare for pursuing the pleasures of the links and the convivial dinners which followed their meetings. Most had their regular caddies who were not only knowledgeable about the links and the idiosyncrasies of their employers but also competent players – some of high standard. For that reason they were occasionally relieved of their ordinary duties to partner their masters in matches, usually by foursomes and sometimes for high stakes. In this way the best golfers among the caddies, clubmakers and ballmakers were sought after as partners and coaches, and the period covered by the late eighteenth and early nineteenth centuries was marked by the emergence of men who, although still belonging to the working class and thus kept in their places by the manners of the time, achieved prominence above their less skilful fellows.

At the same time, as golf became more popular in ever-widening circles, the clubmaking and ballmaking trades also expanded and alongside the player-caddies a number of craftsmen became well-known and successful suppliers of equipment. The most prominent ballmaker at St Andrews at the time was Allan Robertson, who employed several men in his workshop and, being a fine player in good standing with the R and A members, was more often seen with a club in his hand than with one in the vice. His rival at Musselburgh, which by then had become the main links of Edinburgh, was John Gourlay, official ballmaker to several clubs and having a large private clientele. In the eighteenth century a number of clubmakers came to the front, including Simon Cossar of Leith and Henry Mill of St Andrews. Cossar soon established first place and served for many years as clubmaker by appointment to the Honourable Company. Later still James McEwen, who worked as a master wheelwright in Edinburgh, took to making clubs and founded a celebrated dynasty.

The McEwen business was started at Leith in 1770 and was carried on by James's son Peter who married Gourlay's daughter, and their son Douglas. At the turn of the century the McEwens were so well established that they regularly journeyed to St Andrews to sell clubs to the Society members at their spring and autumn meetings. Those journeys, although troublesome and expensive – across the Firth of Forth by sailing boat and across the Kingdom of Fife by horse – were profitable until the rise in St Andrews of a local craftsman, Hugh Philp. He was a joiner by trade but, being in request for the repair of broken clubs, he soon encompassed and perfected the art of making them. Before long he was appointed clubmaker to the St Andrews Society and became famous for his clubs wherever golf was played. He is remembered chiefly for his longheaded wooden putters but he was also celebrated for his iron clubs. They were designed not merely for recovering from rough lies and bunkers, as in earlier days, but for playing the accurate pitch shots and running approaches which, in the absence of proper putting greens, were so necessary for good performances. Robertson, his partner Tom Morris and other good golfers were demanding improved equipment, and the skill of those who worked at bench and forge to supply it improved steadily under the pressure of competition.

While clubs themselves passed through a gradual and systematic development without fundamental alterations in general design the ball underwent a dramatic change in mid-century which revolutionized the game. The introduction of the solid gutta-percha ball in 1848 was greeted with suspicion, antipathy and scorn by the makers of featheries; but the 'guttie', as it was called, succeeded because it was cheaper, more durable, and had the big advantage that when beaten out of shape or cut badly it could be softened in hot water and remoulded as new. Manufacture was ridiculously easy once the simple moulding press was introduced. A rough lump of gutta-percha was inserted in the mould and pressed into a perfect sphere, the mould leaving a pattern on the surface which gave it the necessary aero-dynamic qualities to ensure accurate flight. Many balls could be turned out in the time taken to make two or three featheries, and the guttie became the standard ball for the next fifty years.

None of the ball- and clubmakers of the featherie era could be called a professional golfer and there is no record of any appointment to such a post until just after the introduction of the guttie – an event which led to a quarrel between Robertson and Morris, who had dabbled with the new ball in face of Robertson's adamant opposition. Robertson not only ran a successful business but was also in great request as a partner for R and A members and well able to hold his own in matches. He and others of his stature filled the functions of professionals but the first so described was Morris, who in 1853 was engaged by the newly-formed Prestwick club on the West coast of Scotland. For a modest wage of 15s. a week he maintained the links, and supplemented his earnings by making and selling balls and clubs, coaching beginners and playing with members – a pattern which, apart from greenkeeping, is followed today by the average club professional.

The appointment of Morris can be explained by the difference between the Prestwick club, playing on a private course, and those older ones on the East coast who shared the public links with all comers. At St Andrews, Leith, Musselburgh, Bruntsfield and other centres every citizen enjoyed equal playing rights. The local club- and ballmakers catered for everyone and if they gave preference to their upper-class clients that was in the natural order of things. If the members of the Royal and Ancient Golf Club (which was given that name by William IV in 1834) had possessed a private course they would no doubt have appointed Robertson as professional, but he was probably content to retain independence while at the same time depending considerably on the R and A members for his livelihood. He was by all accounts a pawky player, cunning and shrewd both in his own play and in arranging matches to the best advantage of his side. Short and stocky, he was not the longest of drivers but had a fine, easy, flowing style and obtained results by perfect timing. It has been claimed for him that he was never beaten in a singles match on level terms but apparently he rarely put himself to this test, preferring foursome play in which the responsibility was shared by the partners. He never undertook a serious man-to-man match with Tom Morris. He knew that Tom could cope with him, and Tom was of the same opinion.

Robertson and Morris, in addition to playing foursomes against other professionals for money – Willie Park and the Dunn brothers of North Berwick were among their great rivals – often found themselves on opposing sides as partners for amateurs. The foursome, in which one ball is played on each side, the partners striking alternately, was the most popular form of match, and the result often depended on the performance of the professionals in actual play as well as in the management of the game. In addition to playing their own shots they would also advise their partners on choice of club, direction of stroke and technique of striking. Some of the better players among the caddies would also be called upon in this way, and the entry of a promising performer into the small circle of professionals was achieved then, and remained so for many years afterwards, through the early days spent carrying clubs, watching players good and bad, and gradually developing individual skills. Indeed the twentieth century was well advanced before this pattern underwent any great change.

Robertson had a great and intimate knowledge of the St Andrews links and his stylish, thoughtful play gave him many good scores. He was the first to break eighty at St Andrews and his seventy-nine made in 1859, just before his death, was far better than anything accomplished by the best amateurs and not challenged by any professional for some time afterwards. In those days there was little scope for judging the relative merits of professionals by the acid test of score play with card and pencil. The amateurs had their stroke competitions at seasonal meetings but the professionals were mostly engaged in money matches in which scores were only approximate and rarely recorded. This was all changed by the institution of the Open Championship in 1860 and from that time forth professionals became accustomed to competing in stroke-play competitions organized by clubs and syndicates of amateurs. But Robertson was unable to show his paces in the Open – he died just before it started.

Despite Robertson's respected position at St Andrews he never held the official post of club professional. But when Morris had been at Prestwick for ten years the R and A, who had experimented with the employment of men to keep the links in good condition, decided to make an appointment, and Morris was the obvious choice. He gladly returned to his native city and served the club for nearly forty years.

CHAPTER TWO

The toilers become players

When Tom Morris came back to St Andrews in 1865 he was able to show his fellow-citizens the Prestwick club's Challenge Belt, which he had just won for the third time. He was Open Champion, although the title had not then been accorded. The competition for the Belt, a handsome trophy subscribed for by Prestwick members, was conceived in 1856 as 'A General Golf Tournament for Scotland' and when actually launched in 1860 was confined to eight invited Scottish professionals. In the following year it was rather grandiloquently declared 'open to the world', but the eighteen competitors were all Scots and eight of them amateurs, mostly members of the Prestwick club. Morris's son Young Tommy won the Belt outright in 1870 and there was a lapse of twelve months during which steps were taken to put the event on an official basis. Prestwick, the Honourable Company and the Royal and Ancient combined to provide the present challenge cup, and cannily declared it to be a perpetual trophy. The event was now unquestionably a championship and all earlier winners of the Belt were canonized as ex-champions.

The achievement of a consortium of three clubs in 1872 should have occurred many years earlier, for the original intention of the Prestwick members in 1856 had been to enlist the support of several Scottish clubs and the Royal Blackheath club in London. Unfortunately the clubs had different views and even could not agree when Prestwick proposed to launch the competition at St Andrews in 1857 with each club concerned sending two competitors and paying an entrance fee of £2 for each. This would have provided prizemoney but the conditions had a mixed reception and Prestwick finally decided to proceed independently. So the first competitors, instead of sharing a modest prize fund, played only for the honour of winning the Belt. Even in 1863, when money was offered, it was shared by the second, third and fourth players, and not until 1864 was there a first prize, Morris winning £6.

Although those early promotions were on so modest a scale the Prestwick golfers made a significant contribution to the history and traditions of the game. In addition to inaugurating an event which was to achieve worldwide renown they created conditions which favoured the development of professional golf. Neither consideration, of course, had motivated them. They had no thought for posterity, no inkling that one day their little competition would draw the finest players from the four corners of the earth and spectators in their tens of thousands. The idea of increasing the prestige and social standing of professionals and the wish to do so were equally far from their minds. The professional, whether holding a club appointment or working as a free-lance, was the servant of the amateur, kept firmly in place by the taboos of Victorian times. On the links there was familiarity of a kind. One could not be stiff-necked or standoffish with one's partner, particularly if he was contributing most to the winning of the match by his own play and sage advice. But camaraderie stopped short of the portals of the places where the amateurs gathered convivially after play. So the eight professionals who competed for the Belt in 1860 came to Prestwick virtually unheralded, played their three rounds of the twelve-hole links in one day to complete the thirty-six holes, and departed almost unsung outside Ayrshire.

The minutes of the Prestwick club reveal the casual treatment of the professionals. At the annual meeting held on the previous day the playing conditions were debated and settled by the members. At noon on the day of the competition the players were summoned to hear the conditions, and almost immediately afterwards play began. They had no chance of discussing the arrangements or criticizing the conditions, even if anyone had dared to do so. There were no score-cards and an observer went with each couple to make a record of the strokes and report the totals at the end of each 'round'. The players were there only to compete, and everything else was controlled by amateur officials, without any reference to the men without whom there would have been no competition. Nowadays all aspects of the Championship concerning the professional entrants are decided by the Championship Committee of the R and A, but only in close consultation with the representatives of The Professional Golfers' Association.

After that first championship, in which Willie Park beat Tom Morris by two strokes with a total of 174, the competitors dispersed. Park was duly fêted when he returned to Musselburgh wearing the Belt. Morris went back to his chores at Prestwick regretting his failure to please his members by winning. But neither was conscious of having contributed to the history of the game, although they had laid the foundations of a calling which was to earn the plaudits of the masses and the friendship of patrons in all walks of life. That development was far in the future and for many years after the first Open there was little change in the living conditions of professional golfers and only gradual improvement in their financial and social standing. Not all the competitors in 1860 held club appointments. Morris was attached to the home club and George Brown, the first Scot to be at an English club, was at

Blackheath. Charles Hunter at Prestwick St Nicholas later succeeded Morris at Prestwick itself. Willie Park at Musselburgh counted most of the members of the Honourable Company among his clients but that exclusive club did not employ a professional, a tradition maintained to the present day. Alexander Smith and William Steel, both entered from Bruntsfield, Edinburgh, were also probably free-lances, as was Andrew Strath from St Andrews and Robert Andrew from Perth. They were all alike in their humble roles, dressed unprepossessingly in woollen jackets and reach-me-downs, wearing a variety of headgear from seamen's tarpaulin hats to wool bonnets, and shod in ordinary walking boots innocent of spikes. To judge from a photograph taken at the time they were scarcely distinguishable from the caddies who carried their clubs loose under-arm. The former had carried clubs many times in their careers, and the latter included some likely to become professionals later.

It was the Championship which raised the competitors above their fellows and as it grew in size and prestige so the status of the regular professional improved. But the process was slow and when, twenty-five years later, Sir Walter Simpson, Bart (in *The Art of Golf*) described a golf links as 'a place where rabbits and professionals earn a precarious living', he was not far from the mark. Three years later Horace Hutchinson was to write in the Badminton Library volume on golf:

One can divide into three classes those who derive a precarious subsistence from the game of golf; professional club-makers, professional players who eke out existence by work in the clubmakers' shops, and professional caddies who would be professional players if they played well enough . . . The professional . . . is a feckless, reckless creature . . . He works at odd times, job work or time work, in the shops; but he only does it when reduced to an extremity. If he were ordinarily thrifty he would lay by in the autumn sufficient to carry him through the season of his discontent, when no golf is. He can

lightly earn seven and sixpence a day by playing two rounds
of golf, or, if he does not get an engagement, three and sixpence a day by carrying clubs . . . Many are engaged in a
kind of body-service to their masters at a pound a week,
which usually includes the advantage of a breakfast at their
masters' house and the disadvantage of having to black his
boots. Occasionally they combine with golf-playing more
general branches of industry which they pursue in a spasmodic
fashion. Thus, when we asked one of them whether a brother
professional had no other trade than that of golf, he replied:
'Oh aye! He has that – he breaks stanes.'

Making due allowance for these somewhat facetious
comments we can conjure up a picture of the average
professional of the 1880s, but already the picture was
changing. In the days of which Hutchinson wrote club
committees were concerned primarily with the course
and professional golfers were engaged not as players but
as 'keepers of the green' – in other words custodians of
the links. The duties included supervision of the casual
labour employed on course maintenance, control of
the caddies, attention to the wants of members and
visitors, playing with members when required, and
giving lessons. All this in addition to running the little
workshop behind the clubhouse, where the professional
would work at the bench himself or, in more opulent
cases, direct the work of employees. The most enterprising professionals, of whom Morris, Park and
Robertson were early examples, were keen to develop
on the business side. They also played whenever they
could, but the first to be almost wholly engaged in
playing was probably Morris's son, Young Tommy.
Although he and his brother 'Jof' would have been
required to work in the family shop at St Andrews,
Young Tommy was so clearly a prodigy that he must
have spent more time playing than any of his rivals.
For most of them matches or competitions were activities on the side, not to be compared for steady earnings
with running a golf shop or working at a trade. The

stars of today, on the other hand, make playing their business and leave all commercial affairs to their managers or agents.

Young Tommy Morris was years ahead of his time. At an unusually early age he became accustomed to vying with the best players in the occasional small competitions and when only sixteen astonished everyone by tying with Willie Park and Bob Anderson of Perth in a tournament at Carnoustie, beating both in a play-off. About fifty years later a young Bostonian of eighteen, playing as an amateur, won the United States Open Championship by beating Harry Vardon and Ted Ray, two of the world's finest professionals, in a play-off, and the sensation that caused must have been similar to the shock administered by Young Tommy at Carnoustie. A comparatively untried youngster had beaten two of the best players of the day, but it was no flash in the pan for in the following year the young Scot became Open Champion. He was to win the title four times running, a record which has never been equalled.

How good was Tommy Morris? We can judge only by his performances in the Open and they are conclusive. But let us look at the course on which they were accomplished. The twelve holes at Prestwick were squeezed into so small a space that a modern designer, offered a free hand with the meagre acres, would either refuse the job or recommend a pitch and putt course. The area was bounded on the south by a road to the sea, on the north by a stone wall, inland by the railway line and seawards by an earth rampart. Nine holes of the present links are almost entirely on new ground beyond the wall. The other nine are in the space which accommodated the original twelve, and even those nine are uncomfortably crowded. To assess the situation as it was in the 1870s we have to imagine a sandy waste of hillocks and hollows, clothed with tough sea grass and gorse, and pin-pricked with natural

bunkers mostly in places where no modern course
architect would put them. Fairways in the present-day
sense didn't exist and the putting spaces – they could
not be called greens – were merely level areas of
roughly-scythed grass on which putting as we know it
today must have been difficult if not impossible. Putters
were all lofted clubs, whether of wood or iron, because
it was essential to get the ball airborne at the start of
its bumpy ride. Accuracy as achieved today with the
help of superb equipment, close-shaven greens, well-
kept fairways and properly-designed holes, was impossible on the links a century ago. Another difficulty
at Prestwick was the abundance of blind shots to be
played over forbidding sandhills, for on the other side
the player could find his ball lying well or badly, if he
found it at all. That was the luck of the game and the
pioneers of Prestwick, who founded their club in 1851,
had to make the best of the available land. The twelve
holes varied in length from 100 yards to 570 yards, the
total length being 3723 yards. Taking the length of each
hole and assuming present-day conditions of clubs,
balls, courses and skill, the par for the twelve holes
would be 44. Par is based on the figure which should be
secured at each hole by the average scratch player,
allowing him two putts per green. Any hole over 475
yards is a par five. Any hole 250 yards or less is a par
three. Those in between are all par fours. But in the
1870s such terms as par and bogey, with their attendant
ornithological allusions of birdie, eagle and albatross,
were unknown. There was no yardstick for measuring
the comparative difficulties of golf holes. They were all
difficult and all the best players were inhibited by the
natural hazards and the general unpredictability. All,
that is, except Young Tommy, whose virtuosity is
written in history as recorded by the scores he made
at Prestwick and elsewhere. He created a new record
for the Prestwick links of forty-nine when he won the
championship for the second time, and beat that with

a first round of forty-seven in 1870 when he won the Belt outright with a third successive victory. His thirty-six holes total that year – 149 – was strokes ahead of any winning total achieved in the remaining twenty-two years of the thirty-six holes championship. In fact Tommy himself took seventeen strokes more in winning the new Cup at St Andrews, in very bad weather, and the best score between then and 1892, when the event was extended to seventy-two holes, was 155 by Willie Park Junior in 1889, nineteen years after Morris's 149.

Attempts have been made to assess par for the original Prestwick links and, allowing only for the marked difference in distances obtained by the guttie ball of that time and the modern rubber-core ball propelled by modern clubs, the estimated figure is fifty for the twelve holes. By this rough yardstick Tommy's record of 149 represents one stroke under par for the thirty-six holes. But if we take into consideration the equipment used and the rough playing conditions the splendour of Tommy's game at its peak can be appreciated in its full glory. He was young and vigorous, a dashing player full of fire and confidence, constantly experimenting to improve his game and building with intelligence on the experiences of his elders. He developed what is now the stock-in-trade of the tournament golfer – the controlled approach shot with the iron club hitting down on the ball and imparting backspin to check it on the green after landing. This type of shot when perfected by Tommy and copied by his rivals overcame one of the great difficulties confronting golfers on rough courses – judging a low running shot across uneven ground. Morris introduced such precision into approaching that putting became much easier, and there we have part of the explanation for his fine scores and undoubted superiority. He was probably the first exponent of the art of 'running three shots into two' around the green, at which art we expect all today's

2

stars to be adept. We owe much to Young Tommy in the development of golf techniques and he might have contributed still more to the history of the game but for failing health. Sadly he never again touched the heights after winning the new Cup in 1872. In 1874 he finished second in the Championship and on Christmas Day 1875 he died, aged only twenty-four. His life though short had been eventful and influential. He left his mark on the game and may fairly be described as the first 'playing professional'.

CHAPTER THREE
Into business

Three of the leading Scottish clubs were now associated with the Championship and its prestige increased but it was not yet the most important event. Professionals were still second-class citizens in the eyes of their masters who controlled and observed their activities in a spirit of feudal benevolence. As three clubs shared the responsibility they acted as hosts in turn, and in 1873 the Championship, moving for the first time from Prestwick, was decided at St Andrews. Yet so little was its importance in relation to the amateurs' own competitions that it was fixed for a day immediately after the three-day autumn meeting of the R and A on a links scarred by the mixed efforts of 200 amateurs with varying degrees of skill.

The winner was a St Andrews man, Tom Kidd, who spent more time caddying than playing and never again emerged from the shadows. More substantial winners were Mungo Park, brother of Willie, who returned from a seafaring life to take the title in 1874; and Willie himself, who at last, to the joy of his Musselburgh supporters, won for the fourth time to equal the tally of his old rival Morris. But the heyday of those pioneers was in decline and new men were coming to the fore, who, like Young Tommy, had introduced new ideas and exploited improved techniques. Two of the most successful were Jamie Anderson of St Andrews, who

won three times in succession in 1877, '78 and '79; and
Bob Ferguson, once a caddie at Musselburgh, who
won three times running in 1880, '81 and '82. Anderson,
whose father, a famous character known as 'Old Daw',
had made feather balls for Robertson, was one of
many St Andrews lads who grew up with the game and
played it as and when they could in the streets or odd
spaces, as English boys played football and cricket.
Their implements were rough sticks or old discarded
clubs, and missiles ranged from pebbles to old balls
found on the links or tossed to them by indulgent elders.
Young Jamie, who worked as a clubmaker, became one
of the best golfers in St Andrews, noted for his great
steadiness. He lacked the dash of Young Tommy but
prospered by thoughtful play and application. Ferguson
went within an ace of equalling Young Tommy's
record of four wins in a row, for in the 1883 Championship at Musselburgh he tied with Willie Fernie and
lost the play-off by one stroke when Fernie holed from
the edge of the home green for a two. Fernie, later to
be associated for many years with the Troon club, was
then at Dumfries, but he was a plasterer by trade,
having been apprenticed to that calling on leaving
school. Jack Simpson of Carnoustie, who won in 1885,
was a stonemason, and David Brown (1886) and Jack
Burns (1888) were both plasterers.

In those feckless days the living from golf was so
unreliable and seasonal that the sheet-anchor of a
recognized trade was almost essential. Instead of
hanging about the links waiting for something to turn
up the tradesman-golfer could work at his job until
opportunity offered a round with an amateur or a small
one-day competition, and down tools for the occasion.
There were no plums for professionals. Tournaments
were few in number and modest in rewards – even the
Open Championship was worth only £20 of which half
went to the winner. But the carefree professionals would
travel miles, perhaps using a wagon or cart owned by

one of them, to play for a few pounds and as likely as not spend the winnings in pubs on the way home. It was a shiftless life, as Horace Hutchinson observed, and many strict and upright Scottish parents preferred their sons to be apprenticed to trades, which they could fall back on in hard times, rather than follow the aimless existence of men without roots.

But a name sandwiched between those of Brown and Burns in the championship roll belonged to a man who raised very considerably the status of professional golfers. Willie Park Junior was not alone in the crusade for better things. The wind of change blew others into the battle line during the next decade. But he was the first, and the secret of the success of Willie Park's son was that in addition to the family skill at golf he inherited a keen business sense. Old Willie had been a shrewd and calculating man, more so than his seafaring brother Mungo, and young Willie, better educated, was able to exploit a golfing world insensibly changing in pattern to the advantage of those able and willing to prosper. For example, he was in closer contact with the amateur side of the game and able to deal with it with no sense of inferiority. He won the Open for the second time in 1889 and then, his prestige as a player established, devoted himself to the business side. The quality of his golf suffered, and, unfortunately, his health, but materially he had no cause for complaint. He was particularly successful as a course designer in the modern manner, and the Old Course at Sunningdale, as well as one at Huntercombe and several in the United States, stand as monuments to his skill in making imaginative use of terrain and natural features. But he was also successful in the production and sale of equipment, and in 1897 was able to advertise that he had sold more than 17 000 of his 'patent lofter' clubs at 7s.6d. each. Golf then was indeed very cheap for the amateur, who could equip himself with clubs and a bag for under £2 and buy gutta-percha balls at a shilling each; or, if he were economically inclined, patronize a Musselburgh firm who offered them at 6s.6d. a dozen post free. So Park and Forgan and Morris and other manufacturers in bulk, presumably working on satisfactory profit margins, were cashing in on the tremendous growth in the golfing population. Before 1847 there were only twenty-three clubs in the country and the next thirty years saw the total increase to only seventy-nine. Yet between 1875 and the end of the century it rose to more than 1300. No wonder the professionals with business brains prospered.

During the 1890s when Park and his contemporaries were consolidating their positions, a young man in the south-west of England was building a career in which golf playing and golf business were mingled with excellent results. Although Englishmen began to take up golf in the middle of the century and formed clubs, those clubs had to go to Scotland for professionals. When the gentry of Bideford and Barnstaple started playing, crudely and haphazardly, on Northam Burrows at Westward Ho! in the 1850s, they invited Tom Morris from Prestwick to turn their rough playground into a proper links. After forming the Royal North Devon club in 1864 they again looked to Scotland for a professional and in fact acquired three. Johnny Allan, a St Andrews man, was no sooner appointed than he brought his brothers Jamie and Matt to help in the work, which of course included maintaining the links as well as making clubs and keeping a shop. At that time Scotland was the sole source of manpower but soon after the Allans were installed at Westward Ho! the wife of a working man in the village of Northam, overlooking the links, gave birth to a boy destined to be the first English professional and one of the best of his generation. When John Henry Taylor won the Open at Sandwich in 1894 he was the first non-Scottish professional to take the title. Until then there had been a steady emigration from Scotland by young men eager to exchange the rather precarious living on their own courses for the comparative comfort of a billet with clubs formed by well-to-do Englishmen who required the best equipment and competent coaching. Charles Gibson went from Fife to Westward Ho! in the wake of the Allans and remained there for the rest of his career. Jack Morris, son of George Morris, a brother of Old Tom, became professional at Hoylake after his father had laid out the original nine holes of the Liverpool (later Royal) club. Willie Fernie, plasterer turned golfer, went to Felixstowe when a club was founded there in 1880, and after some years returned to Scotland first at Dumfries and later at Troon, where he was appointed 'greenkeeper, clubmaster and professional'. His first task was to maintain the links, his second to look after the catering and clubhouse services, and his own activities as professional came last in what was the order of priority in those days. Maintenance of the course was of prime importance, and clubs were indifferent to the use their professionals made of their time in keeping shop, teaching and playing, so long as 'the green', as the course was called, was kept in good heart. When Tom Morris returned to St Andrews as professional to the R and A he was expected, for his wage of £50 a year, to supervise work on the links, being allowed the labour of two men two days a week and £20 a year for materials and tools. J. H. Taylor's first job away from Westward Ho! was as greenkeeper-professional at Burnham-on-Sea, Somerset, where he had to contend with the ravages of rabbits and the wind-blown sand which often covered the greens. Even as late as 1896 Margate Golf Club was advertising for 'a ground man, thoroughly acquainted with laying out greens and care of ground generally. *A knowledge of clubmaking not essential.*' (My italics.)

Nevertheless circumstances were changing because playing conditions were improving. The ancient links of Scotland had been made mainly by Nature and required little upkeep because the 'putting greens' were small areas of rough grass cropped by rabbits and the ground between tee and green, which the modern golfer expects to be well-mown fairway, was in practically virginal state. The early caddies, who carried the clubs loose under-arm, were usually required to run ahead of the player to watch for the fall of the ball and guard against loss in the masses of gorse, heather and tangled grass. But as golf became more sophisticated and courses were made by man with recognizable fairways and large greens maintained by machines, greenkeeping gradually became a craft in itself. The new clubs which proliferated in the 1890s found it necessary to have greenkeepers as well as professionals and the professional inevitably rose in status. His duties as clubmaker and repairer, purveyor of balls and other equipment, coach and playing partner for members were sufficiently exacting without having also responsibility for the care of the course.

English golf fed on itself. A club was formed, the members recruited caddies from the working-class neighbourhoods, and the most ambitious caddies were taken into the professionals' shops to learn clubmaking. The best apprentices graduated to a point from which they could strike out on their own, and since new clubs were mushrooming in growth there was no dearth of jobs. In 1900, nine years after Taylor had left Westward Ho! for Burnham, about 300 professionals were attached to English clubs, more than half of them English.

But although many were doing well the lot of the average professional then meant long hours, hard work and modest remuneration. It was no easy way to earn a living but certainly more pleasant than the existence of the average artisan, and a safe billet for one who enjoyed the confidence and respect of his employers. Towards the end of his fifty-four years at the Minehead and West Somerset club Frank Goldsmith must often have recalled with a wry smile the closing years of the nineteenth century, when he struggled to make ends meet. His account book for the first year at Minehead, 1897, showed that he sold a driver for 3s.6d., a brassie for 3s.10d. (to cover the brass sole-plate), and a complete outfit – seven clubs, six balls and a bag – for £2.9s.6d. He received 2s. for playing nine holes and that was no doubt the charge for a lesson.

At about the same time Tom Chisholm was engaged as professional at the Royal Eastbourne club and his contract, or rather his conditions of employment, laid down that he was to keep the club fully informed as to what he was doing, and to be always ready to deal with any problem arising during his working hours, which were defined as 'from early morning until everyone had ceased to use the course for play'. The charges he could make were also strictly controlled – 2s.6d. for giving instruction over eighteen holes, 4s.6d. for a wooden club, 6d. each for balls. Not perhaps the best way to get rich at golf, and in 1901 Chisholm left for the United States and presumably fatter pastures.

Of course such financial relics of the 1890s must be kept in perspective. The history of the Royal Eastbourne club, written by Charles Welsh and from which I quote, also relates that when the members agitated for lower catering charges the cost of a chop lunch was reduced from 1s.9d. to 1s.6d. and whisky from 6d. to 5d. a glass. Long hours and low pay might have been common among professionals eighty years ago, but those who stuck to it had their reward, more often than not, in the pride of a craft well practised and the respect of those for whom they worked. And some, of course, became famous.

Among the 'stickers' one may count Tom Williamson who, just about the same time that Chisholm started at Royal Eastbourne, applied for the job at the Notts Golf Club, in Bulwell Forest, where his sister was working as stewardess and general factotum. The letter offering him the post on a temporary basis provides a vivid illustration of what golf clubs expected from their professionals in those days.

19th March, 1896

Dear Sir,

The Committee of the Notts Golf Club instruct me to say they are willing to engage you temporarily as clubmaker, etc, on the following terms:

1. That you should be at the service (so far as your duties permit) of any member of the Club to play or coach him at a charge of 1s.6d. a round (18 holes), including caddie; same charge to apply to a round (18 holes) on the Ladies' Links whether with a member of the Notts Golf Club or the Ladies Club.

2. That you should take charge of the clubhouse and be responsible for its safety (of course this will not interfere with your sister's duties).

3. That you should take the management of the caddies and the caddies' shelter.

4. That you should conduct the draw on Medal days.

5. That you should assist in keeping the course and greens in order, giving your services upon them for eight hours a week; these hours to be given on such days and at such times as the Committee, or Mr. Griffen on their behalf, may require.

6. That you should receive from the club 5s. a week, commencing from the 29th. February last.

7. That you should take all the profits from making, mending and selling clubs and balls.

8. That this engagement may be determined at any time by 14 days notice on either side.

I want to make it quite clear that the engagement is temporary. Of course it may eventually become of a more permanent nature, but for the present you must be good enough to understand that it is only temporary and experimental, and the Committee will feel themselves at liberty to determine it at any time on giving the above notice.

Please write to me to say if you accept the engagement on these terms.

> Yours truly,
> H. G. Miller,
> Hon. Secretary.

Young Tom Williamson was not appalled by the list of duties or the bleak financial prospects. He accepted the 'temporary' job, it was never formally made permanent, and he remained at the club for fifty-four years, played for England eight times and became an institution in the Midlands.

The formality of the club's letter of appointment contrasts strongly with the casual way in which many men entered professional golf in the nineteenth century. John Steer, who died in 1975 aged eighty-nine, was a founder-member of the PGA and his three brothers also became professionals, but golf in their family started when their father, employed by Sir Philip Sassoon on his estate at Ashley Park, Surrey, was asked to design and make a nine holes course. He had no experience of such work, could use only horsepower and manpower, but it launched him into professional golf and he soon began to make clubs and gutta-percha balls, his wife helping in the workshop. He also took charge of the caddies, as was usual in those days, and proved himself a strict disciplinarian. The boys, issued with armlets made of leather and brass, had to be in clean clothes and boots, or no caddying for them!

Having learned his craft the old man passed it on to his sons and John Steer, who went from Surrey in 1908 to be assistant to Jack Simpson at Lytham, and afterwards became full professional at Blackpool, developed into one of the best-known course designers in the north of England.

CHAPTER FOUR
Coming of the Great Ones

The prolific growth in the number of professionals during the last decade of the nineteenth century inevitably led to several blossoming as leaders, some principally as clubmakers, some primarily as players, and a few enjoying dual reputations. The four outstanding players who began their careers in the 1890s were two Englishmen – J. H. Taylor and Harry Vardon; and two Scots – James Braid and Alexander (Sandy) Herd. In 1905 they were to play a great international foursome over four courses, a test match which aroused great public interest, but long before that they had shown their paces in divers ways and with varying success. Curiously although all four won the Open Championship they did so in inverse ratio to their ages. Taylor, born in 1871, broke through in 1894; Vardon, born in May 1870, came next in 1896; Braid, a few months Vardon's senior, didn't win till 1901; and Herd, the oldest, had to wait till 1902. The likeliest explanation is that Taylor and Vardon graduated from the ranks of the caddies whereas Herd and Braid both achieved distinction as amateurs while working at trades.

Sandy Herd was a golfer from childhood, playing first in the streets of St Andrews, as had Jamie Anderson and many others, using home-made clubs and corks weighted with nails. He might easily have become a professional on leaving school but for the opposition of his parents. With typical Scottish leanings towards caution and righteousness they regarded the calling as 'na guid' and insisted on Sandy learning a trade. So he was apprenticed for four years to a baker and then tied himself for another five years to a plasterer, Baillie Andrew Scott, who was a fellow-member of the St Andrews Golf Club and had previously employed Fernie. All those years Sandy played as an amateur, winning several competitions of the club, to which artisans and tradesmen belonged. He also won a gold medal in an R and A competition for artisans and generally performed so well that, at the end of his time in the plastering trade, he turned professional at the age of twenty-two. After filling one or two seasonal jobs in England he found a secure billet when the Huddersfield club started in 1892.

Because he won only one Open Championship whereas his three rivals had sixteen between them history has placed Herd outside the trio who in their heyday were called the Great Triumvirate. But a study of his record reveals a more flattering picture. In his first season at Huddersfield he tied for second place in the Open at Muirfield, and also won three tournaments which, with first prizes of about £20 each, ranked as major events. He also beat that up-and-coming youngster Harry Vardon in a seventy-two holes home-and-home match at Huddersfield and Bury, where Vardon was professional. In the following year Herd had another brush with Vardon in the final of a knock-out tournament at Portrush, Northern Ireland, and won again. In 1895 he seemed to have the Open title in his pocket when leading by five strokes after three rounds, but was overtaken by a rainstorm and also by Taylor, who started later in better weather. Herd finished third again in 1896 behind Vardon and Taylor, who had tied, and this and many other performances showed clearly that his Open win in

1902 was a distinction too long delayed. He continued to be a thorn in the side of his rivals, being second to Braid in 1910, one stroke behind Vardon and Arnaud Massy (who had tied) in 1911, and runner-up to George Duncan at Deal in 1920. Herd was then fifty-two but there was still a lot of devil in him, for in 1926 he won the match-play championship for the second time. I saw that remarkable performance by a man verging on sixty and was proud to know him as a friend till his death in 1944. He was a warm-hearted man, for all his Fifeshire pawkiness and caution, and particularly well disposed, as might be expected, towards the modern artisan-golfer movement. Although not tall he was sturdily built, very strong, and had one characteristic peculiar to him – a pronounced and prolonged waggle during which his feet would shift rapidly to different positions until he felt himself in the right stance and could then let fly.

Herd's great career overshadowed those of his brothers although all five boys made good as professionals. Fred went to America, won the US Open in 1898, and did well at South Shore Country Club, Chicago, before the homeland called and he returned to be professional at Knebworth in Hertfordshire. Jim and John joined Fred at Chicago and stayed there till they retired. David, who learned clubmaking in Forgan's factory at St Andrews, was professional at Littlestone from 1897 to 1940 and accomplished such good scores in that windswept corner of Kent that one wonders why he never became more prominent in the big competitions. In 1897 he played the links in half a gale from the north-west, the most difficult quarter, in seventy-three, and beat that performance a few months later with seventy-two, ten under bogey. In October 1898, on a much longer course, he went round in seventy-five, again ten under bogey.

Sandy's two sons also became professionals – Alec recently retired from his post at Rickmansworth public course and Bob was attached to the now-defunct Molesey Hurst club near Hampton Court.

James Braid was also a native of the Kingdom of Fife, hailing from Earlsferry, down the coast from St Andrews. At the little fishing village with its natural links he, like Herd, began to play in early boyhood and soon became one of the best players, being scratch at sixteen and a regular prizewinner with the Earlsferry Thistle club. At that time he was passing through his apprenticeship to a joiner, his parents also having insisted on his learning a trade and playing golf purely as a pastime. Braid's work as journeyman joiner took him to various places and at twenty-one he found himself living in Edinburgh and winning many local competitions from a plus handicap. At that time he was probably the most successful artisan amateur in Scotland, but the chance offer of a job in London making golf clubs changed his life. In those days clubmakers were classed as professionals, and young Braid found himself meeting and playing with professionals in the London area. By that time the Royal Liverpool Club at Hoylake and the Royal St Georges at Sandwich had joined the Open Championship consortium and the Open of 1894 was played at Sandwich – for the first time outside Scotland. Braid played and finished ninth. This and other good performances enabled him to become professional at Romford when the club there was started in 1896, and it was in the Romford colours that he won the Open for the first time at Muirfield in 1901. This was the start of a remarkably fruitful decade in his career, for between then and 1911 he won four more Open Championships as well as being runner-up three times, and was match-play champion on four occasions in addition to winning the French title and playing regularly for Scotland against England in the professional international match started in 1903.

Soon after winning the Open for the first time Braid went to Walton Heath where he stayed for forty-five years till his death in 1950. I was privileged to know him for some thirty years and shared the respect and deference which everyone paid to his noble character and profound wisdom. At his prime he was a strong, dashing player, a powerful driver yet sufficiently master of himself to avoid the faults of a mere slogger. He combined length with accuracy to a remarkable degree and in his later years when his eyes were giving him trouble he seemed to find his way round Walton Heath as if by radar. Of course he knew every inch of the ground. On one occasion I went to the Heath to interview him on some matter and was told he was out playing with three elderly members who regularly joined him for a foursome every Monday. I came up with the match just after Braid had driven off and saw his partner surveying the ball which lay in very short heather a foot or so off the fairway. 'I can't remember the last time I saw Braid off the course,' he remarked.

So much for the Scottish side of what I am tempted to call the Great Quadrivium. Since the Scots both came from Fife it would be pleasant to be able to describe the other two as Devonians both, but Vardon was a Channel Islander, born and living all his boyhood at Grouville in Jersey, a few miles from St Helier. For all that the Channel separated their birthplaces the lives of Vardon and Taylor were strangely similar. Both learned golf as caddies, both on leaving school had jobs with golfers who helped them, both went to the United States in the same year, and their sharp rivalry in the Open Championship ended with Taylor a close second when Vardon scored his sixth victory to achieve a record still unequalled. That 1914 success made Vardon on paper superior to Taylor and Braid who each had five wins. But with masters of that calibre scores merely decide which name goes on the trophy, and leave the question of supremacy unanswered. For several cogent reasons Vardon was regarded as the best of his genera-tion, and he had a tremendous influence on the trend

FEATHER BALL, about 1810
Donor – T. Suffern Tailer, Jr

FEATHER BALL, about 1845
Donor – T. Suffern Tailer, Jr

A GOURLAY BALL
MADE PRIOR TO 1850
BY DOUGLAS GOURLAY

DONOR: THE ROYAL MUSSELBURGH GOLF CLUB
EAST LOTHIAN, SCOTLAND
PRESENTED IN 1963

FEATHER BALL, about 1835
Donor – Robert Cunningham

FEATHER BALL, about 1845
Donor – T. Suffern Tailer, Jr

These feather-stuffed balls made in the first half of the nineteenth century show how varied were the sizes and shapes. PGA collection

LEFT: *Evangelists in America. Fred Herd, wearing his US Open Championship medal won in 1898, at Chicago with his brother Jim. With brother John they teamed as pros at South Shore Country Club, Chicago, while brother Sandy was making his way in Britain.* Mary Rowlands

RIGHT: *A famous quartet. The four leading players of their time at St Andrews before the start of their great challenge match in 1905. Standing (left to right): Alexander (Sandy) Herd, J. H. Taylor. Seated (left to right): James Braid, Harry Vardon.* PGA Collection

RIGHT: *Champions both. Sandy Herd (1902) and Jack White (1904) in riper years at St Andrews.* G. M. Cowie, St Andrews

He stood alone against American might in the 1920s. Arthur Havers, Open Champion in 1923, driving at Moor Park, with the majestic clubhouse in the background. Sport and General

Ten men for a boat, to say nothing of the dog. The first Ryder Cup team at Waterloo en route for the United States in 1927: (left to right) George Duncan, Herbert Jolly (half-hidden), Archie Compston, Ted Ray, Fred Robson, Samuel Ryder, George Gadd, Charles Whitcombe, Arthur Havers, Abe Mitchell and George Philpott (manager). Mitchell was taken ill on the train journey, and his place was taken later by Aubrey Boomer. PGA Collection

of golf both in Britain and in the United States. He made two US tours in 1900 which awakened in young Americans an enthusiasm for a new game, and sowed a seed which bore bitter fruit for British golfers in years to come.

There is always scope for speculation on the coincidences of life and how little is needed to divert one's future into quite unexpected channels. No doubt America would have become pre-eminent in golf without the influence of Vardon but one is tempted to wonder how different the history of the game would have been if Vardon, having become, like his father, a gardener, had stuck to spade and fork instead of abandoning them for driver and spoon. The six Vardon brothers were just schoolboys playing cricket and football according to season when the formation of the Royal Jersey Golf Club in 1878 changed life for more than one of them. Harry was then about seven and he and his brothers and chums soon started regular caddying for the gentlemen from England who played a strange game with which they rapidly became familiar. From carrying clubs to using them was but a step and, despite having to use home-made weapons and any missile which came to hand the village boys soon plunged into a competitive atmosphere of their own in which, on the rough common-land near the course, they tested themselves against each other. They were merely following the example of several generations of Scottish boys and in Jersey as in Fife the process threw up some who showed special aptitudes.

On leaving school at thirteen Vardon was employed as a junior gardener by Major Spofforth, a local resident and keen golfer who did much to foster the youngster's ambitions by giving advice, encouragement and equipment. In the event the gallant major lost a gardener and produced a future champion for after some years Vardon, inspired by the fact that an older brother, Tom, was doing well on the mainland as a professional, decided to follow suit. He went first to Ripon, then to Bury before going to Ganton in Yorkshire where he stayed for eight years, during which he won the Open three times. In 1903 he started his long career with the South Herts club and celebrated his arrival in London by winning the Open for the fourth time. Lean years followed caused mainly by ill-health, but he won again in 1911 and 1914 to complete his clutch of six.

Vardon set a new style of play, although in the eyes of some contemporary critics his swing was not without faults. But he had developed a method by sharp observation of golfers good and bad for whom he had caddied as a boy, and history shows how effective it was. He adopted the overlapping grip with both thumbs down the shaft which some late-Victorian golfers had evolved but which became known as the Vardon grip purely because he used it so successfully. He had a much more upright style than most of his contemporaries, and used his large, sensitive hands to swing the clubhead through the ball with easy grace. So smooth were his movements and so calm his temperament that he became a byword for consistency and accuracy. Although not the longest driver among the professionals he was long enough, and his accuracy from the tee and also through the green gave him the edge on his rivals. No one could match him in the long second shots which so often then had to be played with wooden clubs. Although the origins of Taylor and Vardon were strikingly similar their styles and methods were just as strongly contrasted. Vardon had a fairly full, upright swing, a full pivot, mobile feet and a light grip, using clubs which were noticeably lighter than those carried by other men. Taylor, no doubt the stronger player of the two although the shorter, planted both feet firmly on the ground and had a short, punching swing with an open stance. Although not a classic style it was most effective in rough weather and attributable to Taylor's

upbringing on the exposed Northam Burrows, swept by
the Atlantic westerlies. The need at Westward Ho! was
for a low-flying ball and Taylor became adept at
cheating the elements.

The Devonian's pugnacity and tenacity which served
him so well in adult life and in many enterprises, were
derived from his childhood experiences, for he lost his
father when still an infant, and had to leave school at
eleven to work in various ways to help his widowed
mother. Caddying on the links was one obvious way,
but he also worked in the house where lived the great
Horace Hutchinson, twice amateur champion and the
outstanding golf writer of the period. The example of
Hutchinson and his many words of encouragement
helped to inspire the youth with a desire to do well at
golf. He soon became easily the best player among the
members of the Northam Working-Men's Golf Club, but
when a job on the Royal North Devon greenkeeping
staff was on offer he took it and turned his back on
amateur golf. In 1891 he went to Burnham-on-Sea, and
was fairly launched on what was to be a brilliant career.

Building on the meagre education he had received at
the Northam village school, Taylor developed into an
erudite writer and speaker, treating his calling with
pride and his superiors with respect, but never losing
his sense of proportion. His uncompromising attitude to
the task in hand, his determination to succeed and his
enthusiasm for everything connected with golf was far
different from Vardon's calm pursuit of perfection and
philosophic ease of manner. Taylor was inspired by the
will to better himself by application to the business side
of the game, and a desire to protect and enhance the
welfare of his brother professionals. By the one he made
himself successful off the course, and by the other he
ensured a quick rise in the prestige of his calling. He is
remembered not only as a great champion but also as a
good honest man who served his fellows according to
the tenets of his lowly but strict upbringing. I enjoyed

his friendship for forty years till his death at the age of ninety-two, and recall countless occasions on which he showed his worth on and off the course. He did a great deal for himself and his family but much also for the game he loved and adorned.

CHAPTER FIVE
America gets the bug

In addition to witnessing the early rivalry of Vardon and Taylor, the 1890s saw a steady growth in the business side of professional golf. So far most professionals had had only limited scope for selling the clubs and balls they produced, their markets rarely extending beyond the membership of their clubs or the community where they worked. Hugh Philp built up a satisfactory connection as official supplier to the R and A but it was left to his nephew Robert Forgan to expand the business on a much wider front. Carefully trained in the craft by his uncle, young Forgan assumed control in 1852 and decided it was no longer possible to run a viable concern by producing custom-made clubs with his own hands or those of the two or three workmen employed. Expansion of working space and staff was essential, and so well did Forgan plan and work, eventually with the assistance of the future champion, Jamie Anderson, who worked in the Forgan shop for some time, that forty years after he took over the premises hummed with the work of fifty or more men producing five or six hundred clubs a week for selling all over Scotland and to the new English golfers. By that time Tom Morris's shop, close to Forgans, was doing good business of the same kind, as were the Auchterlonies round the corner. Other enterprising producers elsewhere were also foreshadowing the development of the present flourishing clubmaking industry.

In the nineties Willie Park was active in Scotland and later established a London end for his main work of designing courses. At the same time Taylor was beginning a clubmaking business in the south, in partnership with his old school friend, George Cann, who had learned the craft under Charles Gibson at Westward Ho! When Taylor went to Winchester in 1894 Cann joined him and the firm immediately began to prosper, Cann supplying the manufacturing expertise and business drive, and Taylor keeping his name before the public by successes on the links. It was a perfectly satisfactory fusion, founded on an old friendship, and eventually Cann went to the United States to establish an American branch and become professional to the Pittsburgh club. Taylor himself went to America for three months in 1900, following the example of Vardon who, in a tour during the previous winter, had undertaken a tremendous programme of matches against resident professionals in various parts of the country, and did much to foster the development of native American golf. Later that year Vardon went across again to compete in the US Open Championship, in which he beat Taylor by two strokes with the rest nowhere. By that time many Scottish professionals had settled in the States, getting a good income from laying out courses and teaching the growing army of newcomers to the game. Both Englishmen were impressed by the way in which golf, scarcely known to the indigent American ten years earlier, had blossomed with the support of wealthy sportsmen. Taylor himself was offered a valuable contract to stay there but turned it down, and Vardon later confessed that he had been strongly tempted to return to take up 'a more promising appointment' than the post he then held at Ganton.

The early US Open Championships were monopolized by golfers from the Old Country. Willie Dunn, who laid out the Shinnecock Hills course on Long Island for millionaires even then exploiting the connection between golf and real estate, had for father and uncle two of the famous figures of the Morris-Robertson-Park era. The twin brothers Willie and Jamie Dunn of North Berwick opposed Morris and Robertson in one of the greatest matches of the time, played over Musselburgh, St Andrews and North Berwick for £400 a side. Such contests were then decided by courses and the Dunns, after winning easily at Musselburgh, lost the St Andrews match, all then depending on what happened over their home links. They raised local hopes by gaining a useful lead but in the end were beaten by one hole and so lost the whole match, although if it had been decided by holes instead of courses they would have won. Almost immediately afterwards Willie Dunn went to the Royal Blackheath club as professional and greenkeeper. The members then were still playing over Blackheath where James I and his courtiers had golfed a hundred years or more before, and as the heath was public ground with gravel pits and rough tracks among the many natural hazards, the work of maintenance must have been onerous. But Willie prospered for he was soon joined by Jamie and the twins carried on together till Willie returned to North Berwick, where he died in 1880. Of his two sons Willie Junior emigrated to the United States where, in 1894, he beat a fellow-Scot, Willie Campbell, in a match for the unofficial US Championship. The title event was instituted in the following year and Dunn finished second to a nineteen-year-old Englishman, Horace J. Rawlins, who was assistant at Newport, Rhode Island. Rawlins was the second English professional to win a national title, Taylor having been successful at Sandwich in the previous year. History is silent on the subsequent career of Rawlins but Taylor went from strength to strength in Britain and Dunn had a picturesque and generally successful life in the United States.

Visualizing the United States as a productive land

for the enterprising immigrant golfer, more Scots began
to follow their pioneering countrymen. Carnoustie, on
the Tay estuary near Dundee, contributed most to the
exodus and apart from a number of Carnoustie men
who succeeded as players – the Smith brothers Alex,
Willie and Macdonald being among the most prominent – many others found good posts as club professionals, coaches and course designers. The most
celebrated coach was Stewart Maiden, who had much
to do with the early training of Robert Tyre Jones, Jnr,
the world's greatest amateur golfer. The rush of
emigrants was mainly from Scotland for obvious reasons
although, as we have seen, both Vardon and Taylor
had been tempted to remain.

The spread of golf in the United States during the
1890s was typical of the hustling New World and it was
not long before attempts were being made to 'improve'
the game. One innovator named Haskell made history
with an entirely new type of ball which when established revolutionized golf even more effectively than
had the guttie when it supplanted the featherie. Before
Haskell produced his 'rubber-core' there had been
several attempts in Britain and America to improve on
the guttie but the alternatives had all been solid balls
made from a variety of compounds – a mixture of cork
and rubber was one of the most successful – and none
gained lasting favour. Mr Haskell's idea was to wind
rubber thread around a core and case the whole in a
composition cover, moulded as the guttie had been.
When Taylor visited America he was Open Champion
for the third time and, as he related in his autobio-
graphy,* Mr Haskell invited him to try the invention.
Taylor, on the eve of the US Open, felt he would be wise
to stick to the tried and trusted guttie rather than run
the risk of 'swapping horses in mid-stream'. Afterwards
he regretted his caution, because with hindsight he
realized that if he had played the Haskell he would

* *Golf My Life's Work*

almost certainly have beaten Vardon instead of losing by two strokes. It can be anybody's guess what would really have happened because the ball was in an experimental state. But soon improved models crossed the Atlantic to be greeted with general caution by conservative British amateurs and considerable hostility from the professionals who, accustomed to making and remoulding gutties, were not keen to become retailers of the commercially-produced novelties. But progress was not to be checked. Amateurs who could afford the expensive luxuries from America began to play with them, and when Sandy Herd, converted overnight from the aversion he shared with his brother professionals, used them in winning the 1902 Open at Hoylake, the die was cast.

Despite the advancement in reputation and general esteem of Taylor, Vardon, Park, Herd and Braid and other ambitious and dedicated players, professional golf at the turn of the century remained to a great extent in a different world from that of the amateurs. Too many of the fraternity were, as their predecessors had been, feckless and improvident, lacking ambition and drive, and living from day to day with little regard for the future or the need to improve their situation. Their state could usually be traced to their origins as caddies – they were victims of the effects of casual employment on the moral fibre. The caddie, boy or man, had no facilities for making profitable use of his spare time, despite having the will to do so. Periods between jobs were filled with aimless activities which too often led to bad habits and prevented them from earning that respect readily accorded to the industrious and provident.

Unfortunately the professionals who merited that respect could not entirely escape the stigma attached to their calling and lay under a social taboo based on the demarcations of those class-conscious days. Professionals as a body were not regarded as socially acceptable, and the exceptions to the rule could not evade the general inhibition. Taylor himself once told me of an occasion when, as Champion, he played an exhibition match at a well-known London club against another leading player, and both spent the interval eating sandwiches on a bench outside the professional's shop, while the members and visitors they had entertained lunched in the clubhouse. That was no isolated instance; it was typical of the times. The professional could have contact with his members as customers, as pupils, and as playing partners, but there was no question then, nor for long afterwards of his being admitted to the clubhouse except perhaps through the back door into the service regions.

Taylor, who had known hard times at home and left school at an early age, was consumed by a fierce desire to better himself, embracing in that aim the prospects of his fellows. It is probable that from those early experiences and in the knowledge that not even a champion could cross the demarcation line, was born the determination to alter the situation. Henceforth he was to be the champion of deserving causes and succeed in several different ways to ensure the welfare of professional golf and increase the popularity and influence of the game itself. In those closing years of the nineteenth century the dream took shape, soon to become a reality.

CHAPTER SIX
Revolt and organization

As the nineteenth century ended with enthronement as
Champion for the third time Taylor realized that golf
professionals needed an official organization to protect
their interests and co-ordinate their efforts. Taylor and
Vardon, each with three Championships to his credit
in seven years, were the acknowledged leaders, respected not only by their fellows but also by the amateurs
who governed the game. Their rivalry was the most
absorbing topic among golfers in those late Victorian
years. Both competed for the title for the first time in
1893 when Taylor, although having the lowest single
round, seventy-five, finished only tenth with Vardon
much lower in the list. But when Taylor won at Sandwich in 1894 Vardon was fifth and at St Andrews in
1895 he finished ninth behind Taylor after leading the
field on the first round. In 1896, just before the Championship, Vardon beat Taylor in a big challenge match,
and in the Championship itself he tied with the holder
and won the play-off. This duel lapsed for a year
because in 1897 Harold Hilton, very much at home on
his native Hoylake links baked hard by drought, won
for the second time. But that was the end of amateur
victories for nearly thirty years and Hilton's second
win was of less importance, historically, than the
emergence of Braid as a threat to the Vardon-Taylor
monopoly. The tall bony Scot from Elie, who had

recently started his first professional appointment at Romford, went very near to forcing a tie. He had the best round of the week, seventy-four, but Hilton's last round of seventy-five settled the issue. Braid, playing later, fought to the last putt, for he only just missed from four yards for the needed birdie on the home green. In view of the present-day restrictions on the value of amateur prizes and the fact that the only award to the leading amateur in the Championship is a medal, it is interesting to recall that the £40 first prize in 1897 was given to Hilton in the form of plate to that value, and Braid had to be content with the second cash prize of £20. Eighty years ago £40, even in plate, was a good sum for an amateur.

Vardon won the Open for the second time in 1898 at Prestwick and retained the title at Sandwich in 1899. Three victories in four years, uninterrupted by any other professional, made him the talk of the golf world. At that time he was practically unbeatable and although Willie Park ran him close in 1898 the Scot paid dearly for his temerity. Disappointed by his failure Park challenged Vardon to a match and when that came off in the autumn of 1899, after many sharp exchanges over the conditions, Vardon won as he pleased by eleven and ten over seventy-two holes. In the previous year Vardon had beaten Taylor by a large margin in the final of a tournament in Ulster, and at that time the Jersey Islander was firmly in the saddle. His seat, after the two American tours in 1899–1900, was never quite so secure, and in addition to ill-health he had to contend with competition from newcomers. But his natural gifts for accuracy and consistency, linked with his equable temperament, sustained him through a disappointing period and helped towards his still unequalled record of six victories in nineteen years.

The closing years of the nineteenth century were critical times for Taylor in building up his business with George Cann, but his thoughts often turned to the need for creating order in the disturbed world of professional golf. An incident at Sandwich in 1899 showed that professionals were in the mood to combine, even unofficially, in their own interests. Actually the groundswell of revolt had started in 1892 when Willie Park led a protest against removal of the Championship from Musselburgh to Muirfield. Ever since 1874, when three clubs subscribed for the Cup, the event had been decided every third year at Musselburgh, then the home links of the Honourable Company. But when the Gentlemen Golfers of Edinburgh moved to Muirfield they, as promoters of the 1892 Championship, naturally arranged for it to be played on their new course near North Berwick. The decision created anger and disappointment in Musselburgh, for the local tradesmen and professionals feared loss of business and the elders resented the slight on the Honest Toun, as Musselburgh was called. So the citizens, stirred up by Park with his shrewd eye for business, decided to promote their own 'Championship' at Musselburgh on the same days and, exploiting local pride, collected £100 in prizemoney. Now the total money awarded in the 1891 Championship had been less than £30 and the Musselburgh move threatened to upset the applecart, because the Open was not so firmly established as to be proof against competition, particularly when the opposition offered three times the money. So the Honourable Company raised the Open fund to £110, whereupon the Musselburgh faction put off their tournament until just after the Championship. The professionals played for £210 in the two events, and a subtle change had taken place in the relations between them and the Championship clubs.

Nevertheless, despite the obvious desire of the competitors for a progressive increase in the Championship awards the figure hovered around the £100 mark for several more years until, on the eve of the 1899 Championship, a number of players pressed for more and better prizes. There was a strong move towards strike action, but the dissidents failed to get the support of the leading players, despite the fact that the latter had most to gain from a successful protest. Taylor and Vardon, backed by Park and Braid, counselled moderation and the Championship went through as planned, with the promoters agreeing to increase the prizemoney by £30 while stating categorically that if a strike had taken place no increase would have been forthcoming.

The Sandwich incident intensified the need for an organization which could control rebellious elements, make representations to authority, and foster the welfare of professionals. The last aim was the most important because many were living almost from hand to mouth, attached to clubs either too small to pay reasonable retaining fees or provide enough custom, or big enough to exact onerous conditions of employment. Taylor and others were particularly concerned that some clubs were attempting to take over the sale of balls and clubs to their members, putting the profits into club funds and robbing their own professionals of the trade.

During the forty years since the Open Championship started the working conditions of professionals had improved steadily, but not fast enough to satisfy the progressives. When Old Tom Morris took up his appointment with the R and A the guttie ball was in its infancy and not commercially exploited to any great extent. Professionals could make balls in their shops just as they made clubs from raw materials, and both were sold to members who could only be supplied in that way. By the 1890s several firms were making guttie balls of standard quality backed by sales promotion and advertising, and some new types of solid ball were in production. Clubs were no longer being made from primary raw materials, because professionals could buy hickory shafts, persimmon blocks sawn to the rough shape of the heads, and accessories like brass sole-plates and leather grips. In addition several clubmaking firms were doing good wholesale business in the finished product. So the professional, although still spending much of his time at the bench, had become also a purveyor of goods supplied from outside, and that part of his shop devoted to display became as important as the workroom behind. But although the shrewd and astute man with a flair for commerce could profit by maintaining an attractive display, keeping a varied stock and anticipating the needs of his members, there were many less able, lacking business ability or financial solidarity, sometimes both. In some such cases club committees, critical of inadequacy, tried to order goods from suppliers for resale to members.

Such attempts were few and concerned only men who for various reasons were unable to protest. But the desire to protect the weaker brethren and the fear that the practice might spread to the general detriment animated the progressives. No one was keener to defeat this insidious invasion of ancient rights than Taylor, the most articulate of his brethren and an impassioned worker for causes. Later in his long career he was to help form the Artisan Golfers' Association and do splendid pioneer work in the development of public courses, but his first task was to ensure the protection and welfare of his comrades; and there is no doubt that his enthusiasm and energy quickly achieved an end which might otherwise have been long delayed.

Early in 1901 Taylor attended a sporting function at which he opened his heart, on the subject of the moment, to Harold Hilton the famous Hoylake amateur, who had become editor of *Golf Illustrated*. The sequel was a leading article on 22 March appealing for better treatment by golf clubs of their professionals. Taylor was quick to take up the cue he had himself provided. A letter from him in the next issue supported the opinions expressed in the article and invited other professionals 'to come forward and state their views on this important subject'. The next number of the magazine contained a strong letter from Vardon, and contributors to the correspondence columns on 12 April included Braid and Herd. There was also a letter from 'a professional in North Wales', who probably had good reasons for sheltering behind anonymity, stating the time was ripe for professionals 'to band themselves together and form an Association'. One week later 'a North of England Professional' urged Taylor to 'take up the matter and earn the deep gratitude of all'. And on 26 April the North Wales professional returned to the attack by affirming that Taylor was 'by common opinion among all professionals their ideal leader to formulate some such scheme'. He wound up by imploring Taylor to 'come forward and take the bull by the horns.'

Having been accustomed during his youth to dealing with the pot-wallopers' cattle grazing on Northam Burrows Taylor needed no better spur. Now sure of full support he threw himself into the fray with characteristic energy. Wherever he met other professionals he preached the value of organization and was not slow in gaining the interest of outsiders who could help. His most useful contact was with Frank Johnson, a Londoner engaged in the sale of golf goods to professionals, who gave sage advice. Taylor's efforts reached a peak at Muirfield during the Open Championship and the outcome was a meeting at an office in Paternoster Lane, near St Paul's Cathedral. Mr C. Ralph Smith, a great friend of professionals, took the chair and it was unanimously agreed to form 'The London and Counties' Professional Golfers' Association', with membership open to professionals in London and the southeastern counties. Subscriptions were fixed at £1 for professionals and ten shillings for assistants, and it was planned to hold three annual competitions. The fifty professionals present elected Taylor as chairman and a committee to draft a constitution. This had obviously already taken shape in the minds of the leaders and the polishing in committee was done so quickly that fourteen days later, on 23 September, the first annual general meeting passed the result with scarcely any discussion. Mr Johnson was elected Hon. Secretary and it was announced that the Rt Hon. Arthur James Balfour, soon to be Prime Minister, had accepted the office of President.

Arrangements quickly went ahead for the first tournament, a very modest affair but important as a start. It was played at Tooting Bec, south London, on 15 October for £15 in prizemoney and a cup presented by the Tooting Bec club. There were forty-six competitors and Taylor won the Cup and £5 with rounds of seventy-six and seventy-three, total 149. He finished three strokes ahead of Jim Hepburn and Rowland Jones, the latter having the best eighteen holes score, seventy-three. Ernest Jones, later to be famous in the United States as a coach, shared fourth place with Braid and Jack White, each winning £1.6s.8d. There is no longer a Tooting Bec tournament, nor even a Tooting Bec club, but the Cup survives as a memorial of those pioneer days. It is now awarded annually to the PGA member with the lowest single round in the Open Championship.

Although there were already existing bodies representing Midland and Northern professionals, they had been formed mainly for social and sporting reasons, whereas the London and Counties PGA was the direct result of the need for protective organization. It was a success from the start. In just six months from publication of the article which had set the ball rolling an association had been formed, a constitution approved, and a competition decided. No one could say that Taylor and his friends had let the grass grow under their feet.

CHAPTER SEVEN

A great match

Golfers who once played for the customary club stake
of 'a ball' and in these decimalized days risk fifteen
pence in friendly fourball matches should not be too
amused to read that in 1897 a number of Midland
professionals formed a club founded on a competition
for which they subscribed half a crown each for the
winner's prize. Half a crown was a tidy sum in the
1890s but the event was no more than a sweepstake and
was entered into lightheartedly, the suggestion being
made and acted upon over drinks during an interval
at the Empire Music Hall, Birmingham. Among the
pioneers were Charlie Wingate of Olton, his brother
Frank from Harborne, Walter Whiting of Edgbaston,
Lindsay Ross (Sutton Coldfield), George Cawsey
(Worcestershire), W. P. Lewis (Kings Norton) and
H. Waldron. T. Ware (North Worcestershire) won the
kitty when the first competition was played at Edgbaston, but a more important result was the formation of
the Midland Professional Golfers' Club. The principal
objects were social and sporting, and the club was the
earliest known example of the district amateur-
professional alliances which began in the 1920s and now
provide useful winter competition for stay-at-home
professionals.

Walter Whiting was the most interesting character
among those Midland pioneers, being a man of ideas

and, like Taylor, keen to work for the good of his fellows. He was one of seven brothers all professionals, including Fred who, while attached to the Lelant club in Cornwall, gave Jim Barnes, the 1925 Open Champion, his early training. Sam Whiting settled in the United States and another brother was for many years at Royal St George's, Sandwich, where his son Albert is now professional. Walter Whiting was very keen on establishing a national professional golf centre and his son Ray carried on the campaign, suggesting a fixed rota of four Open Championship courses, one each in England, Scotland, Wales and Ireland, with permanent installations and buildings, including an exhibition room and a museum. Some years later Vardon was to advocate a national golf course and similar suggestions have been made from time to time since, coming to fruition, as we shall see, with the great changes of the 1970s.

While Taylor and his Southern comrades were thinking of organization the Midlanders and Northerners were also growing conscious of the need for protecting their welfare and co-operating for mutual benefit. They naturally reacted with interest to the developments in London where, in September 1901, the objects of the London and Counties PGA were spelt out for the first time:

The objects of the Association shall be to promote interest in the game of golf; to protect and advance the mutual and trade interests of all its members; to hold meetings and tournaments periodically for the encouragement of the younger members; to institute a Benevolent Fund for the relief of deserving members; to act as an agency for assisting any professional or clubmaker to obtain employment; and to effect any other objects of a like nature as may be determined from time to time by the Association.

Two months later, following the acceptance of the office of Vice-President by the Duke of Fife, the

Marquess of Granby, Lord Howe, Sir Robert Finlay and Mr C. E. Hambro the banker, the name was changed to 'The Professional Golfers' Association' and the membership opened to professionals and assistants throughout the United Kingdom. When these matters were decided at the first annual meeting on 2 December 1901, with J. H. Taylor in the chair, fifty-nine professionals and eleven assistants were in membership, but the number rapidly increased. A few weeks later Tom Morris, the sage of St Andrews, was made an honorary member, and several vice-captains appointed, including Harry Vardon, Willie Fernie and Willie Park Jnr, all, like Morris, past Open Champions. New members included C. W. Pope (Belfast), G. Goss (Bristol), J. Paxton (Royal Guernsey), Tom Williamson, who had completed five of the fifty-four years he was to serve the Notts Golf Club, and, curiously, J. B. Pettit of Pretoria, South Africa. Those old rivals Andrew Kirkaldy of St Andrews and 'wee' Ben Sayers of North Berwick were elected in February 1902 and Sandy Herd joined soon afterwards. The membership was now so widespread that it was almost a formality for the existing Midland and Northern bodies to join forces with the Southerners. On 25 March 1902, the Midland Professional Golfers' Club decided to amalgamate with the PGA and become the Midland Section. A similar decision was reached by the Northern Counties and the fusions were announced on 18 April, the Northern Counties contributing thirty-eight members and the Midlanders thirty-seven. During the next few months, partly by the amalgamations and partly by natural growth, the total membership increased to about 300 by the end of the year, one-third being assistants. There was also an Irish Section with thirteen members. The PGA had become nationwide and was fairly and squarely on its feet.

Mr Johnson, having launched the administrative side of the venture, retired to concentrate on his business

affairs, and was succeeded as Hon. Secretary by Mr
C. E. Mieville, formerly secretary of Acton Golf Club.
Mr Mieville, who was also elected Hon. Treasurer,
served the PGA faithfully and well in both offices till
illness forced him to give up in 1914. Almost immediately after birth the PGA had to wrestle with the
confusion caused by the introduction of the Haskell
ball and its successful use by Sandy Herd in the 1902
Open Championship. Everyone agreed that the title
was richly deserved and indeed overdue, but many of
his fellow-professionals did not easily shed their instinc-
tive opposition to the new ball. Before the Championship
Sandy had shared their suspicion of the innovation, and
there was tacit agreement to have nothing to do with it.
But Sandy was converted by having the chance to try
a ball during practice, and the rest is history.

The professionals were not alone in their pre-
Championship attitude. Many amateurs felt the Haskell
represented a major departure from what was permis-
sible by custom in golf equipment, forgetting that some
fifty years earlier the guttie had been no less revolutionary and had had a similar reception. In any case
there was no rule in 1902 limiting size and weight, and
no official specification of material and mode of
construction. There was nothing to prevent a golfer
playing a ball made of wood or even resuscitating the
featherie if he didn't mind finishing at the tail of the
field. Nevertheless, the professionals' conservatism was
not easily dissipated. On 3 October 1902, the Midland
Section sent a resolution to the Executive Committee
recommending that the guttie only be used in tournaments promoted by the Association and that 'in the
light of present knowledge' it should be the ball used in
the Open Championship. The suggestion was supported
by the opinion 'that competitors should be on an equal
footing so far as the ball is concerned'.

The weakness of this attitude was patent in the last
few words, implying that the rubber-core ball gave

unfair advantage – therefore it was superior in performance to the guttie. Four days later the Executive
Committee recommended to the annual general meeting that 'only guttie balls be used in tournaments
promoted by the Association'. The Midland rider about
the Open Championship had been dropped, and if the
general meeting on 8 December, with Lord Walter
Gordon-Lennox in the chair, had even considered the
committee's recommendation, its fate was not recorded.
Presumably by that time everyone concerned had
realized that the guttie was a back number and doomed
to the same fate as that befalling the featherie half-a-
century before.

The Midlands implied no animosity against Sandy
Herd, and he was duly elected Captain in succession to
James Braid. Although the Scottish Section had not
then been formed the fact that the twentieth century
had started with two Scottish wins in the Open – after
seven successive English victories – led to a decision to
stage an England v. Scotland team match at the time
of the Open Championship and on the same course.
The inaugural contest at Prestwick in 1903 was won by
Scotland 9–8, and the narrowness of the victory,
tempered in any case by Vardon winning the Championship to make his total four, scarcely justified claims that
the Scots' best players, Braid and Herd, were superior to
their English rivals Vardon and Taylor. In those days
the established means of deciding a question of supremacy was by a serious challenge match, for big stakes
usually put up by interested amateur backers. The
events at Prestwick led inevitably to the great England–
Scottish foursome played in the autumn of 1905,
although by that time there had been signs that the
Big Four were under pressure by newcomers. No other
professional than those four had won the Open during a
period of nine years, but the victory of Jack White at
Sandwich in 1904 hoisted a danger signal. White, who
learned clubmaking with the Dunns at North Berwick

and went south, first to Seaford and then to Sunningdale, was not an unknown quantity, for in 1899 he had
been runner-up to Vardon over the same links. In fact
he had a double reputation, having established a
famous workshop at Sunningdale where he exploited a
rich field among the wealthy golfers of the Surrey
heathland and made beautiful clubs which found their
way to many parts of the world. He had a 'pebble-dash'
voice and a rich Lothian accent. He was also a keen and
efficient businessman and perhaps content to rest on
his laurels as Open Champion for a year. At any rate
he did not repeat his harrying of the Big Four and when
people began to discuss the idea of an international
foursome there was no difficulty in naming Braid and
Herd to represent Scotland.

The idea was no sooner conceived than public
interest began to warm up, soon to come to the boil.
Everyone regarded the contest as a test match, very
different from the exhibition games played on courses
all over the country at week-ends, in different combina-
tions and partnerships. This was to be no ordinary
match, but a real old-time marathon entailing thirty-six
holes on each of four courses – St Andrews and Troon
in Scotland, and St Annes and Deal in England. Mr
George (later Lord) Riddell agreed to back the Scots
for £400 and another newspaper owner, Mr (afterwards
Sir) Edward Hulton, who was based in Manchester,
backed the Englishmen.

By the time the match came off Braid had regained
the Open Championship and he and Herd had all the
better of the first two rounds at St Andrews. This was
not surprising because some ten thousand people
watched the play at close quarters and Scottish crowds,
ever more enthusiastic than English spectators, become
particularly frantic and partisan on such occasions. The
unruly behaviour of the galleries ruffled Vardon, an
easy-going man who hated contention, but it merely
served to intensify the sturdy truculence of Taylor. At

one hole he was shaping up for a shot when a Scot, rather the worse for liquor, stood right in his way and shouted 'Scots wha ha' '. 'Go to Hell', retorted Taylor and played his shot as if nothing had happened. Vardon, less pugnacious, suggested walking off in protest but Taylor said: 'No, Harry, we carry on. They want a damned good hiding.' The Englishmen finished two down on the day but they beat the Scots soundly at Troon a week later, and consolidated their lead so well on English soil that they won the match at Deal by thirteen up and twelve to play over 144 holes.

The match enjoyed tremendous publicity all over Britain for several weeks and undoubtedly did much to increase the popularity of golf, especially since the lively resilient ball was much easier to strike and control than the guttie had been and therefore made the game much less painful and frustrating for the initiate. It is easy to see now that those early years of the twentieth century, marked by the foundation of the PGA, the introduction of a revolutionary ball and the spurt in public interest, had transformed the prospects of professional golf in Britain. From then on not even two world wars could stop the progress towards mid-century affluence and prestige.

CHAPTER EIGHT
The first big tournament

When we survey the world stage of tournament golf, with millions in prizemoney competed for by hundreds of gladiators inured to the pressures and stresses of severe struggles, and followed avidly by millions of watchers on the courses and the television screens, it seems almost ridiculous to recall the welcome given three-quarters of a century earlier for a tournament carrying only £200 in prizes. Yet all the present riches were founded on the good nature and enterprise of two newspaper proprietors, inspired by the wish to help professionals but also with a shrewd regard for publicity, who instituted what was to become the PGA Match-play Championship. How can we assess the value of £200 in 1903 compared with the figure of £25 000 per tournament now expected from British sponsors, except by remembering that in 1903 the average working wage was about £1, and an income of £250 a year represented affluence? Today £5000 scarcely passes muster as a middle-class income, and moreover is subject to taxes of a severity unknown seventy years ago and threatened by inflation which in those times was discussed only by economists.

Few professionals in 1903 had a retaining fee higher than ten shillings a week, and many had none at all. Tuition fees, even for the leading men, were no more than five shillings an hour. The average club subscription was about £3 a year and one could buy a very good wooden club for 12s.6d. or 15s. – prices which gave the professional little profit after he had bought his materials, hickory for the shaft, persimmon for the head, brass for the soles, lead, twine and varnish, and counted a proportion of his clubmaker's wages. It is not difficult therefore to imagine the satisfaction with which PGA members learned that Mr (later Sir) Emsley Carr of *The News of the World* had offered £200 for a match-play tournament. One of the Association's objects was to promote tournaments and several had already been held, but the highest total so far had been £22, and an offer nearly ten times more valuable was so astonishing that we read with amusement if not amazement that the PGA Committee on 27 July accepted the offer 'after careful consideration'. Probably it was the problem of organization which demanded such circumspection by senior professionals feeling their way.

Why did Emsley Carr make this handsome gesture? He was a keen golfer as was his associate Mr George Riddell (as he then was), the owner of Walton Heath. Their newspaper was celebrating its diamond jubilee and was noted for widespread coverage of all sports. But another important reason was the enthusiasm of Taylor. He had just started a series of weekly articles on golf which he wrote for that newspaper for nearly forty years and there can be no doubt that he preached successfully to the proprietors the publicity value of sponsorship. Whatever the influences brought to bear the offer was there, and accepted gratefully. Qualifying competitions in the various sections were arranged to provide thirty-two places in the match-play stages, decided at Sunningdale on 13 to 15 October.

Sixteen places were allotted to the south, five each to the north and Midlands, four to Scotland and two to Ireland. James Braid the winner, who beat Ted Ray in the final, won £100 and there were seven other prizes. Those beaten in the quarter-finals received £10 each but there was nothing for the losers in the first and second rounds. Mr Riddell increased the prizemoney to £240 in the following year to provide fivers for the second-round losers, but the luckless sixteen qualifiers who failed at the first hurdle went home empty-handed. There were no recriminations. The PGA had a worthwhile tournament, the first to be commercially sponsored, and even to qualify for the final stages was a feather in the cap of many an ambitious youngster. The event also aroused interest in parts of the country so far not yet organized. A Welsh Section was formed in August 1904, a West of England Section in May 1909 and an East Anglian Section a few months later.

The nationwide composition of the PGA was complete and the way cleared for other projects, including the idea of a co-operative trading society, first mooted in 1907.

Another sign of growing PGA influence was a decision in 1906 to submit to the clubs running the Championship some suggestions for reorganizing the event which at that time was decided in three days, with a qualifying limit for the last thirty-six holes on the third day. The Association proposed qualifying rounds on the Tuesday and Wednesday to qualify sixty players for the Championship proper, which would be decided on the Friday and the Saturday after a day of rest. Nothing came of this at the time but the proposition was significant as the first attempt by professionals to have a voice in the running of an event which they dominated in actual play. It foreshadowed the amicable arrangement of the present day by which the Association is fully consulted by the R and A Championship Committee on all matters affecting professional competitors.

The idea of a trading society was also premature, for although a detailed scheme was drawn up it had to be shelved because of misgivings about its viability. More than 500 members were invited to take up £1 shares in a Society which would buy from manufacturers and sell to professionals, it being estimated that sufficient profit would be made to pay dividends to the subscribers and an annual bonus to professionals calculated on the amount of their purchases. It was reckoned that there were at least 250 professionals whose purchases would be worth not less than £200 each per annum.

In October 1910 the committee considered the situation in the light of applications for the share capital of £7500 and came to the conclusion that although the scheme was good, and on the surface simple, a business of the kind envisaged would require careful handling and control by men with essential commercial qualifications. It would seem that most professionals at that time were naturally timorous about venturing into business on such a wide front, and it was decided with regret that the time was not ripe. There was some consolation for the pioneers in the decision to hold a trade exhibition at Muirfield during the 1912 Open Championship. This yielded a profit of £20 and was repeated at Hoylake in 1913 and at Prestwick in 1914. Then came the Great War, and four years were to pass before the PGA was able to consider anything save problems of survival.

CHAPTER NINE

America awakes

Jack White's win at Sandwich in the 1904 Open was just another hint to the Big Four that they faced increasing opposition. Edward Ray in reaching the final of the first match-play tournament started a distinguished career which made him Champion in 1912 and American Champion in 1920. He, like Vardon, was born in Jersey but seven years later, in 1877. Ted Ray, as he was always called, was the very opposite of Vardon, having no finesse but plenty of brute force and an uncomplicated free-and-easy attitude to people and situations. Tall and heavily-built, wearing long baggy trousers and a long, loose jacket, with a battered felt hat on his head and a large pipe forever in his mouth, he went into a golf match as an elephant into the jungle. With pipe clenched between his teeth as he crunched into the ball, he bulldozed his way from tee to green with a swaying lunge which would have spelt disaster for any ordinary golfer and certainly found no place in the instruction book. When he connected properly which, to do him justice, was nearly every time, the ball would fly straight a very long way. When his lunging swing was less successful and he landed in trouble it would have been premature for an opponent to fancy his chances, because Ted Ray with a niblick in his hand and the ball in rough country was capable of performing miracles of recovery.

A jovial big-hearted man, he was popular with everyone despite his rough-and-ready exterior and a forcible method of expressing himself. He and Vardon were very close friends – a linking of two opposite natures which could not be entirely explained by the fact that they were born on the same island. They operated in the same county – Vardon at Totteridge and Ray at Oxhey, near Watford – and many times I sat with them and other cronies in a tavern after the day's golf, listening to Ray laying down the law in no uncertain fashion, with emphatic words and puffs of smoke issuing alternatively from his lips; and to the quiet rejoinders of Vardon uttering restrained words of wisdom. Another bond between them was that Ray succeeded Vardon at Ganton when the latter went south. They made two American trips in partnership, and no greater test of amity can be devised than a transatlantic voyage by ocean liner and weeks of travel in a foreign land.

Before Ray reached his full potential the insular world of British golf was shaken by a challenger from France, Arnaud Massy, who in 1907 became the first foreign winner of the Open. Massy and his reputation were well known for he learned the clubmaking craft at North Berwick, married a Scotswoman, and in the previous year had won the first French Open Championship. Born at Biarritz on the Bay of Biscay, where he caddied for British visitors to that fashionable resort, he had been accustomed from boyhood to the Atlantic gales and revelled in the strong winds which blew over Hoylake during that 1907 Championship. A rugged, heavily-built man, typically Basque in his blouse and beret and with his bronzed moustached features, he met the elements with confidence and won the title by two strokes from Taylor who in turn was three strokes ahead of the third man. Massy won the French Open four times and went very near to being British Champion again in 1911, when he had a putt

to beat Vardon on the home green at Sandwich, failed
to hole it, and was well beaten in the play-off.

Massy's feats made British golfers aware that
insularity did not protect them from the consequences of
exporting the game overseas. He was only one of many
straws in the wind of change. For many years the US
Open had been the close preserve of Britons. The
brothers Alex and Willie Smith from Carnoustie won
three times between them; and another Scot, Willie
Anderson from St Andrews, won four times. Fred Herd
of St Andrews was the winner in 1898, anticipating his
brother Sandy's British Open win four years later, and
the 1902 winner was Laurie Auchterlonie, member of a
famous St Andrews clubmaking family, whose brother
Willie had been British champion in 1893. Through
all those years there had been no hint of American-born
talent emerging to challenge immigrant professionals
who had spread all over the States pursuing their
evangelical avocations and mostly prospering more than
their counterparts in the Old Country. But young
America was at the gates ready to reduce the stronghold.
In the US Open of 1909 a young Boston professional,
Tom McNamara, finished second to George Sargent,
an Englishman who beat the Championship record by
four strokes and McNamara by four, thanks to a fine
round of seventy-one completing a total of 290. In 1910
the shadow grew deeper when Johnny McDermott,
another native American, was involved in a triple tie
with Alex Smith and the other Smith brother, Macdonald. Alex won the replay but McDermott was
runner-up and the alarm was ringing loud and clear.
Twelve months later McDermott, victorious in another
triple play-off, became the first home-bred American
winner, and repeated the victory in 1912 with McNamara runner-up.

The real shock was still to come from the hands of
a humble Boston store-clerk who had learned the game
as a caddie, had no intention of playing otherwise than

as an amateur, and entered the 1913 Championship
only because it was being played on his doorstep at the
Brookline Country Club. In three extraordinary days
this obscure young amateur of twenty climbed to the
heights, and began a distinguished career. He was
destined to play for his country many times and be
captain of several Walker Cup teams as well as the
first foreigner to be elected Captain of the Royal and
Ancient Golf Club. But in 1913 no thought of future
renown was in the mind of Francis Ouimet, a tall
gangling awkward young man with modest ideas about
his prospects in the Championship. There were two
powerful reasons for modesty because the consensus was
that the Championship lay between Ray, the reigning
British Champion and Vardon, then five times Open
Champion and a past winner of the US title. A tie
between the two Englishmen was a logical outcome
and they duly tied, but young Ouimet, playing in a
rainstorm, came with a rush at the finish to join them.
The fairy story ended in character on the following day
when Ouimet returned a seventy-two to beat Vardon
by five strokes and Ray by six in a historic play-off.

There was another twenty-year-old in that field at
Brookline who attracted considerable attention, first
because he made a self-confident début in big golf
which astonished his more experienced rivals, accustomed as they were to brash young Americans; and
later because he finished fourth, only three strokes
behind those who tied. It was the start of a career
which was to make Walter Hagen the most successful
as well as the most discussed professional of his time.
Twelve months later he won the US title, and after the
war strode in his cocksure way over links on both sides
of the Atlantic and in many other parts of the world;
mostly winning, sometimes losing, but never forgoing
his place in golfing history as the greatest showman of
them all.

CHAPTER TEN
End of an era

When Walter Hagen became a champion at twenty-one on 21 August 1914, the Great War had begun and all thoughts of sporting fame gave place in Britain to patriotic fervour and the urge to fight and work for victory. Since the war was to carve so deep a gulf between the old times and the new it was fitting that the last great golfing occasion before the holocaust saw the climax of the triangular tussle which had been waged for so many years by Vardon, Braid and Taylor. They approached the 1914 Championship at Prestwick on level terms, each having won the title five times. Braid had done so in ten years from 1901 to 1910, Vardon in sixteen years from 1896 to 1911, and Taylor in twenty, having won his first Open in 1894 and his last in 1913. All three were in their forties and while girding themselves for yet another struggle must also have realized that the time was approaching for them to give way to ambitious youth. They knew that time was running out, but did not suspect that the 1914 Championship would be the last for six years. Yet a few days before they went to Prestwick the die had been cast by an unknown youth in a far-off Serbian city. On 28 June the Archduke Francis Ferdinand of Austria and his wife were assassinated in the streets of Sarajevo, and a crime which seemed at the time to be just another Balkan incident was to draw all Europe and finally most of the world into the maelstrom of total war.

Neither the huge crowds who flocked on to the
Prestwick links in those hot sunny days of early July,
nor the golfers who were to entertain them in a memorable contest, had any foreboding. The spectators sensed
only the importance of the golfing occasion, and asked
only two questions – would the Great Triumvirate
resist the challenge of youth and, if so, who would be
the winner. The 1913 Championship at Hoylake,
where Taylor had scored his fifth victory by eight
strokes from Ted Ray, with Vardon another stroke
behind, seemed to suggest that the younger generation
still had some way to go, for the Hoylake field had
included not only the best young Britons but also
interesting and menacing invaders. McDermott, the
US Champion and his compatriot McNamara had
crossed the Atlantic to be the first all-American
professional challengers for the ancient title. And
Massy was accompanied by two very good young
Frenchmen, Jean Gassiat, holder of the French Open
title, and Louis Tellier. Of those only McDermott, who
finished fifth after a very good first round, made any
real impression, and the hopes of the others were
swept away in a gale of wind and rain which battered
the exposed links on the final day. Taylor had always
been capable of mastering the most boisterous conditions, and he went on his determined way, hitting
low-flying drives through the wind. He was doubly
lucky that week, for he had to hole a six-foot putt on
the home green to survive the qualifying stage, and the
wind was his friend at the finish.

McDermott did not contest the 1914 Open but the
Prestwick field included four Britons who were to have
much to do with titles and tournaments in the post-war
years – George Duncan, Abe Mitchell, and Ernest and
Charles Whitcombe, who after the war were joined by
Reginald Whitcombe to make a celebrated golfing
brotherhood. Charles Whitcombe was only seventeen
when, in 1913, he and Ernest both qualified for the

final stages of the match-play tournament at Walton Heath. As it happened both brothers fell in succession to Duncan, who reached the final and then accomplished the almost impossible by beating James Braid on Braid's own course. This was probably the clearest indication so far that the days of the Triumvirate were numbered, although not the first evidence of Duncan's ability. In the previous year he had finished fourth in the Open, and in the match-play finals of 1910 he had beaten Braid and Taylor before losing to Herd in the final. Born in Aberdeen, one of a large family, he had followed the usual pattern of the time by caddying on the local links, learning to play by imitation, and holding several minor professional jobs before, like many another Scot, moving south – to the Hanger Hill club in north London.

Mitchell, rival as well as friend of Duncan, had a different early career, learning his golf as a member of the Cantelupe Artisans at Forest Row, Sussex, and developing wrists and arms of steel by his work as gardener and forester. He was the acknowledged best player at Forest Row, played for England against Scotland three times, and had a distinguished amateur career which ended in 1912 when he lost to John Ball at the thirty-eighth hole in the Amateur Championship final at Westward Ho!, giving the famous Hoylake player his eighth victory. Mitchell turned professional soon afterwards and quickly made his mark although, with him as with Duncan, the Whitcombes and many others, the hiatus of war lost valuable years.

As with their careers, so with their styles and attitudes – widely different. Duncan was temperamental, explosive in argument, often dogmatic, always at his best in a challenging situation, quick-witted and quick-playing. Mitchell had a quiet reticent manner, typical of one reared in the Sussex Weald and accustomed to the regularity of Nature's cycle. He was strong physically, wielding his driver like a whiplash, and few could even hope to hold their own with him from the tee. But he was weak in temperament, given overmuch to worry about his golf, too prone to wilt under pressure – indeed, so unsuited psychologically to the life of a tournament professional that many successes were achieved only because he was an outstanding golfer. He had many fine performances to his credit but failed to win the biggest prize – the Open Championship – because the prospect of victory played havoc with his nerves.

Duncan on the contrary had nerves of steel, no fear of anything or anybody, and an abounding confidence in his own ability. Although he considered he had modelled his style on that of Vardon, he certainly never emulated Vardon's measured rhythm. Speed was built into Duncan as it is into a motor-car and this was particularly evident on the putting green. A quick look at the line, a rapid one-two in the address, placing the clubhead first in front and then behind the ball, and a firm stroke, all in such rapid succession that it was really one combined movement. He usually struck short putts with sidespin, believing this made the ball hold the line better.

Mitchell the nervy introvert and Duncan the cocky extrovert were foils to each other and united by a bond of genuine friendship which their equally genuine rivalry did not disrupt. For several years they sustained a partnership, sharing their prizemoney, and Duncan never ceased to admire Mitchell's great powers while bemoaning the man's inability to do himself justice on great occasions. They were in the 1920s what Vardon and Taylor had been in the 1890s. But the 1920s were a long way off as the scene was set for the last great battle of the giants.

After two rounds at Prestwick it seemed that the expected triangular contest had become a duel, for Vardon was leading the field and Taylor by two strokes with Braid not in real contention. The fight

between the two Englishmen was given added drama
by the fact that, by the luck of the draw, they were
paired for the last two rounds. Nowadays, under the
'leaders out last' system, they would no doubt have
played together, but there was no artificial draw in 1914.
It was just chance that brought them together, a
chance which was to have a sad outcome for Taylor.
At first all went well for him. In the third round,
profiting by Vardon's weak putting, he returned
seventy-four against seventy-eight to turn a deficit of
two into a lead of two, and when he gained another
stroke at the opening hole of the final round he had
every reason to feel satisfied. But by that time the
galleries, large enough in the morning, had been swollen
by many late arrivals and some ten thousand people
were on the congested links, most of them with eyes
only for the two Englishmen. Not surprisingly Taylor
was more affected by the turmoil than the imperturb-
able Vardon, who could not have been cooler. He
recovered one of the lost strokes at the third hole and
regained the lead at the fourth where Taylor, having
already been upset by a clicking camera on the third
tee, bunkered his drive and put the recovery shot into
the burn. The hole cost him seven, Vardon scored a
copybook four to go ahead, and went on almost
placidly, in comparison with his shattered rival, to win
his sixth Open by three strokes. Braid, never really in
the battle, finished ten strokes behind Vardon, who
was left on a pinnacle rather like an Olympic gold
medallist, with his friends and rivals flanking him at
slightly lower levels. The war made that 1914 Championship their joint swansong but it was a stirring tune
on which to finish their brilliant careers as champions.
All three had given much to golf in various ways and
were to go on doing good work for the game and their
comrades for a long time to come. But there was to be
no more championship golf in Europe for six years, as
more serious matters claimed attention.

CHAPTER ELEVEN
In and out of war

War came with startling suddenness to disturb the national euphoria induced by ten years of Edwardian foreign policy following the mainly peaceful years of Victoria's reign. The Crimean War involving regular soldiers scarcely touched the ordinary public, for all the horrors. The South African War called many volunteers into action and therefore had a greater impact on family life, but it was still too remote to affect the daily round in Britain or prevent projects like the formation of The Professional Golfers' Association. But the Great War affected almost everyone in one way or another and golf was hit harder than some other sports owing to difficulties arising from shortage of equipment and transport problems. Many PGA members joined the Forces or left their shops to work on the land or in war factories. Similarly, the majority of club members were dispersed over land and water. The autumn tournament programme of 1914 was cancelled, including the match-play Championship, now worth considerably more than the original £200.

For the Association itself the disruption came at a critical time. It was a growing organization depending vitally on a regular subscription income, which hitherto had sufficed merely to keep the finances healthy. There had been no scope for accumulating solid reserves, and the small surplus available when war started was soon exhausted as the subscription revenue decreased progressively. At one stage indeed the locker was bare and only a generous gesture by a good friend, inspired by none other than Ted Ray, saved the situation.

No one would have thought of casting bluff, hearty pipe-smoking Ray in the role of diplomat and fund-raiser. He was not accustomed to choose words to suit the company or with the intention of impressing people for an ulterior motive. He called a spade a spade and sometimes something else. One of many stories told of him concerned a spectator who approached him after an exhibition match with the question: 'How can I drive a longer ball?' ' 'It it a bloody sight 'arder, mate', was the instant reply. Perhaps Ray's down-to-earth approach was more effective than a silver tongue, for he managed to persuade the Earl of Wilton to come to the rescue with a gift of £500.

A few weeks later the war was over and the Association faced the years of peace with confidence. But the years of war had taken toll. Mr F. H. Brown, who had become secretary early in 1914 on the retirement of Mr Mieville, enlisted in the Honourable Artillery Company in the following September and died on active service. Many of the younger members joined in the rush to enlist and some of them, too, did not return. Charles Mayo of Burhill and George Duncan thought it would be a good idea for PGA members to keep together and a 'Niblick Brigade' served with the 2nd Company, the Rifle Brigade at Winchester. The others, at that time all bachelors, were A. G. Steward (Beckenham), Albert Styles (Croham Hurst), W. Tomlinson (Cooden Beach), A. Macey (Littlehampton), H. E. Kirby (Verulam), G. W. Robertson (Burhill), J. Seager (South Staffs), H. Bruton (Eltham), Jack Hood (Lowestoft), A. Smith (Leicester), Albert Tingey (Woodcote Park), Walter Mayo (Burhill), W. Eastland (South Herts), H. Amos (Burhill), H. Line (Maidenhead), T. McRae (Flackwell Heath), H. Shoesmith (Thorpe Hall), W. Starbeck (Burnham & Berrow), E. Evans (Burnham & Berrow), Herbert Jolly (Foxgrove), T. Jolly (Woodside), P. E. Rosser (Richmond), H. Reveley (Sunderland) and C. Westermann (Ealing).

Duncan eventually served in the Royal Flying Corps and survived to celebrate peace by winning the first post-war Open. Charles Mayo went to the United States in 1919 but most other survivors stayed in Britain, including Herbert Jolly, who spent the last part of the war as a musketry instructor and later played in the first Ryder Cup match; and Tingey, who became professional at Frinton-on-Sea and was for many years Secretary of the East Anglian Section. He was the chief correspondent of the Niblick Brigade, and one of his early communiqués to PGA headquarters painted a picture of a recruit's life which the modern soldier would regard as a horror story:

We get up every morning at 5.30 and those sleeping in barracks have to be in bed by 10 p.m. We get two slices of bread and butter and one pint of tea for breakfast; meat, peas and potatoes (unskinned) for dinner; and one pint of tea, one slice of bread and butter and one slice of cake at teatime; and occasionally apples and bananas.

There are seven drills a day and a five-mile route march every other day. We have all had to rough it, but there has been no grumbling amongst the PGA boys, for we all made up our minds to stick it and not complain.

Such a diet would be regarded today as starvation fare, certainly meagre preparation for five drills a day and three route marches a week. And there was no NAAFI in those days to help fill odd corners. There was only one consolation – apparently no spud-bashing!

When Mr Brown joined up Mr W. Penman stood in as caretaker secretary, and on his resignation in February 1919 a solicitor, Mr Robert Perrins, became secretary to tackle the difficult work of reconstruction.

It was typical of the optimism in the PGA camp that within a few short months the Association had started a Journal and rented a modest suite of offices in Ethelburga House, Bishopsgate, where for the next forty years many momentous decisions were made and a tremendous amount of work done by a small but devoted staff. Since the formation of the Association the administration had been conducted by honorary officers using their own homes or offices, and the establishment of proper headquarters marked a significant advance in the importance of professional golf.

It was merely a coincidence that a few weeks later there was evidence of a distinct change in the relations between the PGA and the clubs promoting the Open Championship. A conference to discuss arrangements for the 1920 revival was attended in June by delegates from the six clubs – the R and A, the Honourable Company, Prestwick, Royal Liverpool, Royal St George's (Sandwich) and Royal Cinque Ports (Deal) and the Association. Several times before the war the PGA had suggested changes in the Championship format but had been ignored, although the proposals were usually adopted later. The different attitude in 1919 was due partly to a general change in social climate as a result of the war, partly to the need for advice from those having practical experience, and partly to a realization by the clubs that the time for private promotion had passed.

One of the drawbacks of the pre-war arrangement was that although the six clubs were technically jointly responsible, each Championship was organized and controlled by the host club, and this naturally caused widely different circumstances according to the venue and the attitude of the local officials. In December 1919 the promoting clubs met in Edinburgh and asked the Royal and Ancient Golf Club to accept the sole management of the Championship, the delegates agreeing that 'the time had now arrived when there should be a supreme ruling authority for the management and control of the game'. This led to the formation of the R and A Championship Committee which since then has worked to bring the Championship to its present lofty status as a world prestige event. The Committee also assumed control of the Amateur Championship but the significance of the change from the professionals' point of view was that the new regime, while carrying on for many years the seigneurial stance of pre-war days, was more prepared than the clubs had been to consider the interests of professional competitors. From that time forth the relations between the PGA and the R and A developed on amicable and co-operative lines to the benefit of both bodies.

Although the war ended in November 1918 it was deemed impracticable to revive the Open Championship in 1919. Demobilization was slow, and time was also needed for bringing championship links into condition. But there was consolation from another quarter for professionals back from war duties and eager for serious competition. For several years the *Daily Mail*, inspired by its dynamic owner Lord Northcliffe, had achieved publicity by sponsoring various competitions attracting popular interest; and Lord Northcliffe, who owned the North Foreland course on the Kent coast, was a keen golfer. Both factors combined to provide £500 for a seventy-two holes Victory tournament at St Andrews, open to all available professionals who had qualified for the final stages of the 1914 Open. The event was regarded as an unofficial Open, and could not have been more keenly contested, although the level of scoring reflected the rustiness of celebrated swings and the condition of an Old Course still suffering from wartime neglect. The outcome confirmed the general view that Duncan and Mitchell were natural successors to the Great Triumvirate for they tied at 312, sharing the prizemoney and taking their scores in an exhibition match, played on the Eden Course on the following day, to decide who should have the gold medal. Mitchell was successful with seventy-seven against seventy-nine and as he beat Duncan later that year in the final of the match-play tournament, he could look back on his first post-war season with great satisfaction.

There were bright prospects, too, for the Association. In addition to the Earl of Winton's gift for the general fund they received almost as big a boost for the benevolent fund. The war had scarcely ended when speculative builders in London, animated by the profit motive rather than any desire to implement the Government's promise of 'a land fit for heroes to live in', began to cover the suburban fair acres with bricks and mortar. Courses laid out on leasehold land fell easy victims to the building boom and one of the first to go was Acton Golf Club, where Josh Taylor, brother of John Henry, was professional. How much the Taylor charm worked in that case isn't known but the Acton trustees gave all the club's assets, eventually realizing nearly £500, to the PGA Benevolent Fund.

The walls of the new offices at Ethelburga House reflected justifiably optimistic smiles as 1920 dawned. From then on, until the next war, it was to be peace with progress.

CHAPTER TWELVE

Uncle Sam supreme

While the PGA was moving into top gear again a much newer organization on the other side of the Atlantic was finding its early life a little complicated. The decision to form a Professional Golfers' Association in the United States seemed to be a good one in January 1916. American neutrality was being maintained with popular support and American industry was profiting by the production of arms and materials for the Allies. As public affluence grew the number of golfers and courses increased and the club professionals, many of them by now indigent Americans, were ready for incorporation. They had no need to combine because their welfare was threatened, as the British pioneers had feared in 1901, for the average American club professional in 1916 was on a much more democratic footing with his amateur employers, who left him to conduct his business in his own way. In many cases he was virtually manager of the club, having overall supervision of greenkeeping and catering in addition to supplying golf equipment and teaching the game. But there were other reasons for organization, and the chance came when Rodman Wanamaker, heir of the New York store millionaire, offered 2500 dollars for a knock-out tournament to be run on the lines of Britain's *News of the World* event, and suggested the formation of a national body to promote it. As with the British PGA progress was rapid once the decision was taken. A constitution was drafted and approved at a meeting in New York on 24 February 1916, and the USPGA was in business, with eighty-two founder members. From those modest beginnings sprouted the huge organization which now dominates American professional golf and controls 7000 members and a tournament schedule worth nearly nine million dollars a year. But in 1916 despite the fact that the *fons et origo* of the new body was a tournament, the general emphasis was on the welfare of the members, for in those days, although a few professionals like Hagen, McDermott, Jim Barnes and Macdonald Smith were playing as well as fulfilling the more humdrum duties of club professionals, there was no hint whatever of the riches to come, or even of anything approaching a schedule of tournaments. As with the British PGA and the match-play tournament, the Wanamaker event was for a long time isolated, and not until after the war was there any distinct move towards anything more. Another of the many similarities between the two PGAs in the early days was that the Wanamaker match-play event was modelled on *News of the World* lines, with district qualifying rounds providing a restricted field for the knock-out stages. But the USPGA was born under a malignant star, for America entered the war in April 1917 and the first Wanamaker tournament, won in October 1916 by Jim Barnes, the Cornish-American, was followed by a gap of two years during which Americans had other and more serious objectives.

Despite their affinity in aims and objects and methods of working there was a distinct contrast between the two Associations in their relations with the amateur side of the game – a contrast so marked that the Americans who came over by ocean liner for the first post-war Open at Deal were astounded by what seemed to them archaic conditions. They found the social cleavage so wide that the professional competitors were not allowed inside the Royal Cinque Ports clubhouse and were provided with meagre and crowded changing facilities in the professional's shop. The amateur competitors, of course, were able to use the club's locker rooms. This was normal practice in Britain although one significant pointer to possibly better relations had been provided in the previous summer when PGA representatives went to St Andrews to confer with the Championship clubs on the arrangements for the Open. The conference was held in the R and A clubhouse and the PGA delegates were the first professionals to pass through the main door into the rooms of the premier club. But they were in mufti and on official business!

The home professionals at Deal accepted what was for them the usual arrangement, but the Americans were very critical, particularly Hagen who, as reigning US Champion, regarded the situation as insulting. He had his own characteristic way of expressing disgust – he changed in the hired car which brought him to the course, in sight of the windows of the building from which he was excluded. The gesture was typical of a man who even then was creating a reputation for showmanship, but the last laugh was not with him, for he finished fifty-fifth in a field of eighty-one, leaving long Jim Barnes to carry the Stars and Stripes into sixth place.

British golfers finished the first post-war Open in command, but the story of the week was the sensational last-day collapse of Mitchell and the brilliant recovery by Duncan. Following his 1919 successes Mitchell was the man of the moment and more than fulfilled expectations when he followed a first round of seventy-four with a seventy-three to lead by six strokes from Barnes and Sandy Herd at half-way. Duncan, the logical challenger, looked right out of it with 160 for thirty-six holes, thirteen strokes behind. But the very fact that Mitchell was so far in front created a psychological problem for him. He slept badly and had to wait until midday before starting his third round, wondering all the time what his rivals were doing on the course. As luck would have it he was just preparing to start when he saw Duncan coming to the last hole and learned that he was certain to finish with a low score. The sequel was a hooked drive which landed Mitchell in trouble and he went completely to pieces in a round of eighty-four. Moreover Duncan had gone round in seventy-one so in eighteen holes the gap of thirteen strokes had been wiped out. Mitchell recovered his nerve to some extent with a fourth round of seventy-six, but Duncan was round for the last time in seventy-two and won the title by two strokes from Herd with Ted Ray another stroke behind and the unfortunate Mitchell no better than fourth. Although he achieved many good performances during the next few years Mitchell never finished in the first three in the Open. That 1920 Championship was the high spot of Duncan's career, too, although he went very near to a famous victory in 1922 by making one of the brilliant recoveries for which he was famous. But by that time British professionals were waging mainly a losing battle with the Americans. In the thirteen years from 1921 to 1933 the Open was won only once by a non-American – Arthur Havers in 1923.

What had happened since 1912, when victory for a home-bred American in the US Open was a novelty, to make American golfers masters of the international field? The primary cause was the influence of immigrant Scots who taught the game to young sport-loving enthusiasts who improved on the lessons to become better than their masters. A wider territory, allowing golf to be played somewhere in America all the year round, and a larger population were contributory factors, and there was also the undeniable truth that Americans matured quicker than their British contemporaries and possessed, by their cosmopolitan inheritance, a greater capacity for application and a finer competitive sense. These ingredients demanded a catalyst and it came with Ouimet's sensational performance in that 1913 Championship. It made golf front-page news and a topic for street-corner gossip. Thousands of Americans for whom baseball was the national game suddenly became aware of golf and were fired with the desire to emulate Ouimet. If an apparently frail, gangling youngster of twenty could singe the beards of great performers like Vardon and Ray – why, the sky was the limit!

If Vardon's 1900 tours sowed the seeds of America's eventual golf supremacy, Ouimet's win was the fertilizer which brought the plant to maturity. That first post-war American challenge for the Open Championship at Deal ended in failure, but in 1921 Jock Hutchison, born in St Andrews, and in the American, won the title at St Andrews, and in the following year Hagen made amends for his previous failures by becoming champion at Sandwich, despite a desperate last round of sixty-eight by Duncan which brought the mercurial Scot to within one stroke of Hagen's score. Following Havers's win at Troon there was a mournful string of ten American victories – three more for Hagen, three for the great amateur Robert Tyre Jones and one each for Barnes, Tommy Armour, Gene Sarazen and Densmore Shute. The rot was stopped in 1934 by Henry Cotton, who was to rank as Britain's number one golfer for nearly two decades, and although the United States continued to turn out fine golfers they were subject to pressure from other countries as professional golf, after the 1939–45 War, became worldwide in action and influence.

CHAPTER THIRTEEN
An eye to business

One of the most far-reaching steps taken by British professionals in the early post-war years was the incorporation on 23 January 1921, of the Professional Golfers' Co-operative Association Ltd. The idea, conceived in 1907, had taken fourteen years to germinate, but in the meantime there had been significant changes in the circumstances of professionals and in their business attitudes. In 1910 fewer than 100 progressives had supported the proposal, and with the great majority expressing little or no interest it had been shelved. The war created still further delay but afterwards the climate was favourable and the concept more ambitious. Whereas originally it had been planned to have initial capital of £7500 in £1 shares with only fifty per cent called up in the first instance, the PGCA Ltd was floated with a capital of £10 000 represented by 2000 shares of £5 each.

The original shareholders were Ted Ray (20), W. L. Ritchie (10), Jack Ross (10), J. M. W. Thomson (10), W. G. Oke (5), R. McKenzie (2) and R. Perrins (1). Jimmy Thomson was appointed manager – a first choice by those who knew him as the foremost figure in the growing business of providing trading links between manufacturers and professionals. The single share was allotted to Mr Perrins in his secretarial capacity. The other founders were all running successful

4

businesses at their clubs. George Oke, Devon-born, was
then at Honor Oak Park and later at Fulwell (where
seventeen-year-old Henry Cotton began his apprentice-
ship as Oke's assistant) and had a flourishing export
trade in handmade clubs; and Willie Ritchie (Worples-
don and later Addington), Bob McKenzie (Stanmore),
and Jack Ross were all Scots who had sought and found
their fortunes in the London area. McKenzie, who
later served for many years as chairman of the PGA,
once told me of his arrival in the capital, a teenager
making his first long journey from home (he was born
at Nairn in 1882) to be assistant to James Braid at
Romford. He expected to have to make his own way
from King's Cross, but Braid was on the platform to
greet him and take him to his 'digs'. That was just one
of many gestures by a true Scottish gentleman who
spoke words of wisdom when he spoke at all, and held
out many a helping hand to those in need.

Ritchie, also at one time assistant to Braid, was
born in Aberdeen in 1884 and inherited an exquisite
taste for old Highland malt whisky. He always kept a
precious bottle in his little office at the back of the
Addington shop, and I well remember the stern reproof
administered to an uneducated Sassenach when, having
been invited for the first time to take a dram, I looked
round for some means of diluting the generous tot. Jack
Ross, born at St Andrews in 1871, held posts at Seaford,
Ipswich, Banstead Downs and Newport (Mon.). Ted
Ray, who subscribed £100, was the magician who
charmed the Earl of Winton on behalf of PGA funds
during the war.

All those men and 300 others who, in the short
space of two months, raised £7000 of the required
capital, were practitioners in clubmaking. Some
worked alone in their modest shops but the majority
employed one or more clubmakers and in a number of
cases operated miniature factories. But changes were
on the way. Steel shafts had been tried in the United

States in 1914 and declared illegal, but the post-war shortage of hickory and the threatened brake on progress at a time of expansion forced the United States Golf Association to legalize steel in 1926. British clubmakers fought a rearguard action for several years but it was a losing battle. When steel shafts became legal in America the R and A canvassed PGA opinion, which was against a similar move in Britain as detrimental to the business of professionals. But the march of events went on remorselessly until, in November, 1929 the R and A legalized steel shafts without consulting the PGA. By then, of course, everyone in the clubmaking industry realized that the steel age had arrived, and in retrospect it can be seen that the gloomy fears of 1926 had been unfounded. The art of clubmaking by hand steadily declined without becoming extinct, the expert clubmaker went from shop workbench to factory floor, and the club professional became even more a purveyor rather than a producer.

Such changes were to have a decided influence on the careers of professionals skilful enough to play for the best prizes. Release from the tyranny of the bench gave them more scope for competition just as important tournaments were increasing in number. The creation of more incentives increased the enthusiasm of players and the consequent publicity widened the general interest in golf. It was becoming a regular topic for sports writers and a correspondent of the *Westminster Gazette*, after the 1921 Open, published the first British 'averages', sixteen years before the institution of the PGA's own classification for the Harry Vardon trophy. In the unofficial 1921 table a minimum of fifteen rounds qualified and Joe Kirkwood, the Australian-American famous for his trick-shot exhibitions, gained first place with an average of seventy-four 9/25ths, Arthur Havers being second and Ted Ray third. Jock Hutchison, winner of the Open, did not play enough rounds to qualify, but had an average of seventy-two 7/9ths for nine rounds. The table was significant as showing a dramatic increase in the tournament programme. The field for the ambitious player was widening, although years were to elapse before conditions would favour renunciation of all other professional activities.

The PGA, whose founders had laid emphasis on the objects of welfare and benevolence while visualizing two or three tournaments 'for the encouragement of the younger members', was on the way to a two-tier organization. By 1924 the membership had topped 1000, the revenue had reached four figures, and the members were getting very good value for a modest subscription. Five big tournaments worth together £5000 were in the programme, with more to come. At this juncture Robert Perrins, who had done so much to achieve this state of affairs, and had carried on through a period of ill-health, was obliged to resign. His place was taken by brother Percy, who found himself in the secretarial chair at a time of change, with the younger members eager for tournament play, holding views different from those of their elders who had started as clubmakers and still believed the Association should be concerned mainly with the business side and the welfare of members. Conservative opinions prevailed both at Executive Committee meetings and at annual general meetings, for the proxy vote was then in force and proxies in the hands of district representatives opposed to change were sufficient to defeat the younger and more progressive elements.

When H. le Fleming Shepherd, Secretary of Moor Park club, conceived the idea of a 'Target Golf' competition with the laudable object of improving standards in approach play, it was taken up by a London newspaper, the *Evening Standard*. Points were scored by players according to how close to the hole their shots finished, each green being marked by concentric circles – the Target. Instead of welcoming this innovation the PGA refused official recognition because the field was to be limited to seventy-two invited players, and the policy was that every member, no matter his standing as a player, had the right to compete in a recognized event. Even twelve years later, when the makers of the Penfold ball planned a league tournament in which twelve leading players would meet each other, the Association would not include the event among those held 'under PGA auspices'. Nowadays there is willing co-operation with several sponsors who limit their entries, for the good reason that every competition helps professional golf and it is better for the PGA to be involved in the promotion than to stay aloof and have no control.

Although there were arguments about 'restricted' tournaments and other matters the membership was wholly behind the officers in various attempts to improve the status of professionals and in particular the conditions under which they competed in the Open Championship. Relations with the Championship Committee were amicable enough but the Championship clubs themselves were reluctant to depart from the custom which made their clubhouses out of bounds for professional competitors, and in the more democratic post-war climate professionals became increasingly unwilling to submit to such treatment. The groundswell of revolt soon made itself felt. The PGA had a major victory before the 1925 Open, when an approach was made to the Prestwick club seeking inside dressing accommodation for the professional competitors who, in previous Championships there, had been barred from the clubhouse and had to change in a marquee. Many of the older Prestwick members still saw no reason for a relaxation of the rule, but the Championship sub-committee agreed with the PGA, and one of the locker-rooms was reserved for professionals.

That Championship also influenced future policy in another way, for immense and unruly crowds of spectators swarmed on to the confined links on the final day, and the chaos was directly responsible for the tragic collapse of the Scottish-American Macdonald Smith, a native of Carnoustie, who seemed to be a certain winner until the spectators, running wild, jostled him to defeat in their efforts to cheer him home. The Championship, won by Cornish-born Jim Barnes, was the last in which such links were open to all free of charge. Stung to protest by the disorder, the PGA campaigned for control by admission charges, which were duly imposed in the following year for both Open and Amateur Championships. Vardon, who had experienced very similar conditions at Prestwick in 1914 when winning his sixth Open, was particularly critical of the use of archaic and unsuitable links on which crowd control was difficult. He proposed a plan for a national golf course with stands or vantage points and a charge for admission, the proceeds, after deduction of expenses, to go to the competitors. This was prophetic stuff, for although spectator-stands were many years ahead, gatemoney was charged at Lytham in 1926. But alas for Vardon's hopes, the balance sheet issued by the R and A held no joy for the professionals. The net takings at Lytham amounted to £962, which was devoted to 'reducing the deficit standing against the Open Championship account'.

CHAPTER FOURTEEN

A British revival

The 1926 Championship was preceded by district qualifying rounds in an attempt to deal with the ever-increasing entries which rendered 'on-the-spot' qualifying difficult. This was agreed at a meeting between the R and A Championship Committee and the PGA, represented by J. H. Taylor, John Rowe, Arthur Haskins and Albert Wheildon, and three sectional competitions were held for North, Centre and South, with overseas entrants allotted to each section in proportion to entries. The experiment was not repeated but provided one historic event, Bobby Jones's virtuoso effort in the Southern Section at Sunningdale, where he scored sixty-six and sixty-eight as a preliminary to winning the title at Lytham. Of more lasting importance was that the innovation was indirectly responsible for the institution of the Ryder Cup series. Overseas entrants, because of the need for qualifying (in those days no player, not even the Open Champion, was exempt) had to be in Britain for two or three weeks prior to the Championship itself, and a professional international match between the United States and Great Britain was played at Wentworth. It was a repetition of a match at Gleneagles in 1921 when Great Britain won by $10\frac{1}{2}$ points to $4\frac{1}{2}$. That contest was notable as the last appearance of the Great Triumvirate in an international contest, and Vardon and Braid won their singles against Tom Kerrigan and C. Hackney, Taylor being narrowly beaten by Fred McLeod, the US Champion of 1908. But the march of time was shown by Duncan and Mitchell holding the posts of honour, Duncan beating Jock Hutchison, who shortly afterwards won the Open, and Mitchell halving with the redoubtable Walter Hagen. What seemed to be a vast superiority of Britain over America was emphasized at Wentworth in 1926 when the home side won by $13\frac{1}{2}$ points to $1\frac{1}{2}$, with Mitchell beating Jim Barnes, the Open Champion, by eight and seven and Duncan defeating Hagen six and five over thirty-six holes. But each of those pre-Ryder matches was contested by Americans immediately after a long sea voyage, with their eyes on the Championship. As we were to see so often afterwards the invaders, when the chips were down and they were acclimatized, almost invariably triumphed.

The most striking example of this American capacity for keeping the main end in view was provided by Hagen when, soon after landing in Britain in 1928 with the aim of regaining the Open title, he was involved in a seventy-two holes challenge match with Archie Compston, the rugged Midlander who, in his aggressive way, was as courageous and resourceful as the suave American. H. le Fleming Shepherd, who was Secretary at Moor Park at the time, was criticized in some quarters for suggesting Compston as the man 'to put Hagen in his place', in preference to the more obvious choice of Duncan. But Hagen was only a faint shadow of his true self, Compston became more and more ruthless as the match went steadily in his favour and Hagen suffered the biggest reverse ever dealt a professional in such an engagement. Only one hole of the fourth round was required to settle the match, with Compston winner by eighteen and seventeen, but for the sake of the crowd they played the remaining seventeen holes and Compston won that little match as well. Yet what happened in the Open at Sandwich a few weeks later? Hagen first, Compston third!

However much the outcome of the Wentworth international match was discounted by subsequent events, the occasion was historic, because Duncan, then the professional there, took advantage of the euphoria created by the victory to persuade Samuel Ryder, who was employing Mitchell as a private coach, to promise a cup for an official match. Mr Ryder had a flourishing seed and herb business at St Albans and was keen to help professional golf, although sceptical about the publicity value for himself. I was there during the preliminary discussions and remember him expressing doubt whether any Press comment would link his name with his business. The late Laurence Cade, a Fleet Street colleague, wagered to the contrary and of course won the bet.

Actually the news did not cause a tremendous stir at the time and the calm atmosphere of Ethelburga House was scarcely ruffled. Indeed the inaugural match at Worcester, Massachusetts, in 1927 was regarded by the PGA as secondary to the mass attack made by the British players on the US Open Championship. The problem of financing the trip was solved by a fund launched by *Golf Illustrated* which realized £3000, and the editor, George Philpott, son of a professional, managed the British team. Although Ryder's gesture was generally appreciated the 100 guineas gold trophy was not endowed, and this fact gave PGA officials headaches for some years. Money was not the only difficulty. Neither the PGA ranks nor Ethelburga House could provide a manager for the 1931 match at Scioto, Ohio, and Fred Pignon, a golf writer very popular with the professionals, accepted the job. He did so at some personal sacrifice for the news agency employing him refused leave of absence and Fred took his annual holiday for the purpose. Fred did a fine job but he was an 'outsider', as Philpott had been, and the appointment emphasized the rather detached attitude of PGA officials towards the competitive side in those days.

The second match at Moortown in 1929 had been won by Britain, with Duncan the captain beating Hagen the American captain by ten and eight; and when we squared the series at Southport and Ainsdale in 1933 there seemed to be no reason why the two countries should not continue on more or less level terms. But victory at Southport had depended on a missed putt on the home green by Densmore Shute, who made amends by winning the subsequent Open at St Andrews, and nearly a quarter of a century passed before Britain won the Cup again.

The early Ryder Cup matches brought into prominence several post-war products of British professional golf, including Archie Compston, the Whitcombe brothers, Aubrey Boomer, Fred Robson, and a coming star destined to shine brilliantly for many years – Henry Cotton. He was only twenty-two when he played at Moortown and gained his first big success by beating Al Watrous four and three. It was unfortunate for Britain that his second appearance was delayed for eight years, first by a difference with the PGA causing him to refuse inclusion in the team for Scioto, and later by his appointment at Waterloo, Brussels, from 1933 to 1936, for only home-born players domiciled in their native country could take part. Percy Alliss's appointment to a Berlin club at about the same time was another deprivation that Britain could ill-afford.

Cotton was not only the most successful British professional of his time but also a trend-setter. Nowadays for a well-educated youngster of the middle classes to turn professional is no novelty, but Cotton's decision to do so at seventeen – he was the son of a prosperous business man and product of a distinguished London school – was a new departure. It signified his determination to make good at the game by learning all he could about making clubs and using them. He went first to George Oke at Fulwell and after similar appointments as assistant at Rye and Cannes obtained his first full professional job at nineteen at Langley Park, Beckenham. Soon afterwards he went under his own steam to play on the winter circuit in America, covered his expenses and returned well primed with experience of American methods and conditions. He forced himself to the top by hard work and devotion, assisted by an alert mind and an exceptional capacity for analysis, and by his example and performance helped to put professional golf on the road to its present world-wide prestige.

The year of our second Ryder Cup victory marked a turning point in the affairs of the PGA. Percy Perrins, who had run the office with earnest ability for eight years, was obliged to retire, as his brother had been, and in February, 1934 the reins were taken up by Commander R. C. T. Roe, a retired Royal Navy officer, who was to use them for twenty-eight years to guide the Association into realms undreamt-of by the pioneers. He had been on active service throughout the Great War and brought to his new job tremendous energy, a flair for leadership, a gift for organization, and an urge to improve the image of professional golf. It is primarily to him that tournament golfers of the present day owe the material benefits they enjoy, for he can indeed be called the father of the British circuit.

A few months after Charles Roe arrived at Ethel-burga House another significant event occurred – Henry Cotton won the Open at Sandwich by a virtuoso display of low scoring, and ended a sombre period of thirteen years during which the Open had been won twelve times by Americans. The deep depression among spectators was shared by golf writers at St Andrews when we had to make frantic transfers of sleeper reservations from Friday to Saturday night and spent a rain-filled day watching two Americans, Denny Shute and Craig Wood, play off for the title – over thirty-six holes. The skies seemed to weep in sympathy with the spectators. But, as the old song sang, when night is darkest dawn is nearest. At Sandwich twelve months later the sun shone on a glorious revival of British fortunes, the larks heralded a brilliant Cotton victory, and Alfred Perry, Alfred Padgham, Reggie Whitcombe and Dick Burton, as well as Cotton himself, carried on the good work during the remaining post-war years.

All this had an immense effect on the importance of professional golf and naturally inspired increased sponsorship for prizemoney tournaments. In 1936, largely through the efforts of Fred Pignon, who had joined the *Daily Mail*, that newspaper revived a tournament which had lapsed for some years and offered £2000 – a record sum at the time and equivalent I suppose to the present-day minimum of £15 000. In the same year the Silver King and *News Chronicle* tournaments were started, each with £1000. For several years Mr A. E. Penfold had been in the promotional field on behalf of the golf ball he manufactured, and with Dunlop continuing their Southport tournament, started in 1931, the British programme was taking shape as a 'circuit'. This received its accolade in 1937 with the institution of the Vardon Trophy for the most successful golfer of the year. The bronze statuette of the great man, executed by Hal Ludlow, a well-known artist and a good golfer, was won for the first time by Charles Whitcombe with an average of 71.62 strokes for twenty-four rounds. If circumstances had remained normal beyond the 1939 season the circuit would have expanded faster than it did. But not many weeks after Burton's victory at St Andrews the world was plunged once more into war.

CHAPTER FIFTEEN

At war again

A look back to the 1930s will show that although
the development of tournament golf and the successes
of home professionals in the Championship made the
biggest public relations impact, the domestic affairs of
the PGA were also prospering. The continued support
of many distinguished well-wishers, and in particular
the close interest of Royalty, gave much satisfaction
during a period when the sons of George V were keen
players and patrons. Edward Prince of Wales was one
of the most-travelled golfers of his time, for on his many
tours abroad he neglected no opportunity of playing or
at least talking about the game, while at home his
appearances in public as player or spectator were
occasions for popular interest verging on hysteria. When
he arrived on the Southport and Ainsdale course in
Lancashire to watch the 1933 Ryder Cup match there
were record crowds swollen by many thousands who
knew nothing about golf but wanted to see the Prince.
He was then President of the PGA and on his accession
as Edward VIII in 1936 he consented to become
Patron, his brother the Duke of York succeeding him
as President. On his accession as George VI the Duke
became Patron in turn and his daughter, Elizabeth II,
similarly honoured the PGA when she ascended the
throne. In that way royal recognition of golf, which
had suffered only short eclipses since early Stuart times
was sustained, although it was regretted not only by

professionals that the game no longer attracted royal participants.

On the strictly business side there was a change in management of the Professional Golfers' Co-operative Association following the death of Jimmy Thomson in July 1934, aged fifty-one, shortly after being elected an honorary member of the PGA. Manager and a director of the PGCA since the formation in 1921, he had built a flourishing business with much benefit for the shareholders. Jimmy Thomson had endeared himself to all with whom he had dealings, for although an able business man and a hard worker, he was also humane, endowed with a generous and kindly spirit. A loss of that kind is usually not easy to sustain but the PGCA shareholders were fortunate in that a natural successor was available. George Gibson was appointed manager in November 1934 and brought his own personality and business acumen to the task of carrying on the work of a long-standing friend. It was to Jimmy Thomson, indeed, that he owed the start of his long connection with the golf trade.

Son of William Gibson of Kinghorn, Fife, founder of a successful clubmaking business, he was apprenticed to banking and later went to Montreal as cashier in the Royal Bank of Canada. He returned on the death of his father in 1921 and Thomson persuaded him to stay in Britain and enter the golf business, for which he was fitted by his family history and banking experience. In January 1922 he started as a traveller for A. G. Spalding & Bros and was therefore well versed in the business and aware of the problems and needs of professionals when he began his reign at the PGCA. It was to last more than thirty years and be marked by several important milestones, including the achievement of a million-pound turnover in 1960. That peak would have been scaled earlier but for world events, for during the remainder of the 1930s the clouds of war gathered again.

For many years the Open Championship had been preceded on the Saturday by a professional match between England and Scotland, but the increasing importance of the Open made the leading players unwilling to have such a distraction from the task of preparing for the major event. The England–Scotland match at Sandwich in June 1938 was the last in a series started in 1903, and its place was taken, later that year, by a four-cornered international tournament in which Ireland and Wales also had teams. The venture was ill-starred for while the professionals were playing at Llandudno trenches were being dug in London's parks and Hitler's aggression was the news of the day. And by the time in 1939 when the Llandudno experiment should have been repeated the storm had burst and Britain was once more at war.

Charles Roe had been recalled by the Admiralty some time before hostilities began but fortunately was stationed at Chatham and able to keep an eye on PGA affairs with the help of his very able assistant, Miss Cockburn. But they could do nothing to ease the plight of members attached to Continental clubs who had to make hurried and in some cases adventurous journeys to the homeland. There was no time to dispose of their stocks or settle their affairs, and Wally Marks had to leave the Waterloo club at Brussels with only the clothes he wore. Competitive golf came to a virtual standstill, and the *News of the World* finals scheduled for late September were abandoned. As the PGA Journal, *The British Golfer*, was suspended for the duration members were kept informed by a news-letter typed, duplicated and circulated by Miss Cockburn, who worked mainly at home, visiting the office twice a week to deal with the mail.

The Association's finances were in better shape than during World War I and this was just as well, because activities were severely restricted. Many members joined the Forces or were called up as reservists, and a large number volunteered for police, fire brigade, civil defence and other non-combatant roles. No fewer than 935 members, well over half the total membership, served the country in various ways. Of the 664 in the fighting services twenty-seven were killed, twenty-seven taken prisoner, and twenty-three invalided out.

Those PGA members who remained with their clubs were beset by problems of supply. It was not long before manufacturing restrictions and shortage of materials dried up the output of golf balls and other equipment. Even the drive for food production hit many clubs, some losing their courses entirely for the duration and others seeing one or more holes fall under the plough. A drop in subscription revenue for the PGA was inevitable. The subscription for wartime was reduced to 10s. for professionals and 5s. for assistants, and those serving in the fighting forces were excused all payment. But the loyalty of members was equal to the challenge. More than eighty of those serving insisted in paying their dues, and some 200 others continued to pay at the peacetime rates in the effort to maintain finances in a healthy state.

By the end of 1941 the production of golf balls had ceased and the remoulding of old covers was halted for a while by a regulation in November 1942 forbidding the use of controlled material for that purpose. Then the manufacturers developed a method of remoulding which was within the regulation and for the rest of the war and for some time afterwards golfers existed on remoulds and jealously-guarded pre-war stocks. Scarcity of equipment was a minor hardship in a conflict which seared through the whole community. But even the horrors and privations of war had to end, and with peace another chapter in the PGA story began. Commander Roe returned to Ethelburga House, potato fields became fairways once more, the professionals came back to their shops, and the work of reorganization began.

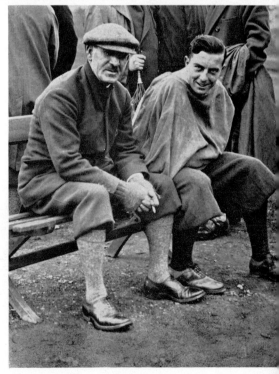

ABOVE: *March to victory.*
Archie Compston steps forward
as Walter Hagen putts on the
first green at Moor Park –
beaten 18 and 17 in their 72
holes challenge match in 1928.
Three weeks later Hagen was
Open Champion for the third
time! H. le Fleming
Shepherd

RIGHT: *Eager youth and*
ripe experience. Abe Mitchell
with mittens and Henry Cotton
with improvised windcheater,
waiting before starting play in
one of the early Roehampton
tournaments. Today's stars
dodge the wind by chasing the
sun. Sport and General

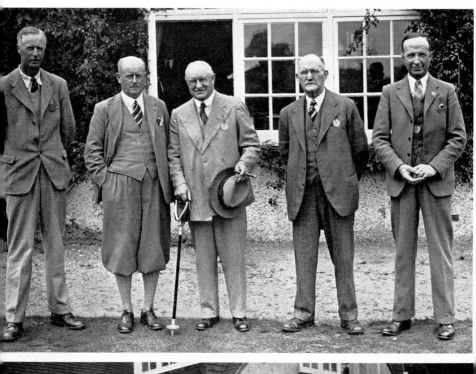

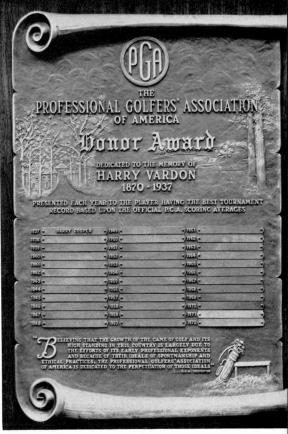

OPPOSITE TOP: *Sir Emsley Carr, who started the PGA match-play championship in 1903, flanked by (left to right) C. K. Cotton, James Bradbeer, J. H. Taylor and Commander R. C. T. Roe, at Oxhey in 1936.* PGA Collection

OPPOSITE: *The start of a great career. Dai Rees, far right, listening to J. H. Taylor during the prize-giving ceremony at Oxhey in 1936 after winning the PGA match-play championship. Next to him is Ernest Whitcombe, the runner-up.* PGA Collection

ABOVE LEFT: *The Master in bronze. The Harry Vardon Memorial Trophy awarded each year to the leader in the Order of Merit.* Associated Press Photo

ABOVE RIGHT: *America honours a great Briton. The Honor Award of the USPGA, instituted in 1937, the year of Harry Vardon's death, to commemorate the six times Open Champion.* PGA Collection

'Mine age is even as nothing.' James Sherlock, 82, and George Duncan, 73, prancing off the first tee at Fulwell to compete in the Teacher Senior Championship in 1957. Sport and General

Despite the obvious difficulties there was intense activity at Ethelburga House. Even before the war ended Charles Roe, in periodic visits to the office, had been making preliminary arrangements for a resumption of tournaments, and on 28 May 1945, the month in which the war with Germany ended, a sub-committee composed of Bob McKenzie, Henry Cotton, Charles Johns, George Oke and Arthur Wheildon met to plan a programme. They were able to count on several sponsors, all newspaper proprietors. The *News of the World* put on a VE match-play tournament at Walton Heath, the *News Chronicle* and the *Star* provided £3000 for two separate events, the *Daily Mail* planned a stroke-play tournament for St Andrews and the *Daily Sketch* sponsored a four-ball competition at Fulwell, Middlesex.

The Walton Heath revival was contested by 149 professionals and produced a surprise winner in Reg Horne, then attached to a modest nine holes course in Hampshire but destined to profit by a breakthrough which marked the start of a distinguished career. The St Andrews tournament, played in the autumn after VJ day, attracted 172 entrants of whom six were Americans, including Lloyd Mangrum, playing in uniform. The winner, however, was British, Charlie Ward beating Max Faulkner by one stroke. In this impressive way the curtain came down on an unexpectedly successful 1945 season. Prizemoney had totalled £7575, a remarkable achievement in the face of many difficulties.

Apart from carrying through all the promotional work Charles Roe and Miss Cockburn were busy at Ethelburga House on general administration, including the task of tracing missing members and finding jobs for many who returned from service to find themselves without appointments. Gradually the employment situation improved, and there was no doubt about the expansion of the tournament programme. There was

also further evidence of the close co-operation between
the R and A and the PGA, for in December McKenzie,
Roe and Cotton went to St Andrews to discuss with the
Championship Committee arrangements for the first
post-war Open. 'Your delegates', wrote Commander
Roe in the Bulletin, 'were received in an extremely
friendly manner and their views asked for and acted
upon.' Soon afterwards a sub-committee drew up a
programme of twelve major events for 1946, in addition
to the Open and the Irish Open, carrying £25 463 in
prizemoney, easily a record.

At the PGA Annual General Meeting at St Andrews
during Open Championship week Lord Wardington
was elected President in succession to the Duke of
Kent, who had died in an air crash on active service.
Another election gave membership to Bobby Locke,
which he celebrated by winning two tournaments and
taking the Harry Vardon Trophy as well as leading the
averages with 73.00. And at the end of the first full-
scale post-war season honour was done to the man who
had started it all. John Henry Taylor was elected an
honorary life member, fifty-two years after winning the
Open for the first time. Three years later both Taylor
and James Braid were elected vice-presidents, the first
professionals to receive this distinction.

The regular annual increase in the number and
value of tournaments and growing public interest
demanded progressive improvement in organization
and ancillary facilities. This was dictated not only by
the need to cater for and inform spectators, but also by
the pressure of sponsors who set much higher standards
of promotion than in pre-war years. The first PGA
scoreboard appeared, numbered armbands for caddies
were introduced, as well as other innovations to make
golf a spectacle to be enjoyed in comfort. In 1949 the
PGA had a big test when the Ryder Cup match was
played at Ganton, and although the week was a
triumph of promotion for which the Ganton club, the

PGA and Scarborough Corporation shared the credit, it ended disappointingly for Britain. The home players won the foursomes 3–1 but were overwhelmed in the singles by some brilliant scoring by the Americans. The match, which Scarborough had guaranteed for £5000 yielded a profit of £2686 for the Ryder Cup Fund, and the accounts for 1948–9 also showed a profit of £345 on the General Fund and a surplus of £475 on the Tournament Fund. The membership had risen to 1425, including 325 assistants.

It was with a real sense of achievement, therefore, that members attended with their guests the first post-war dinner at Grosvenor House Hotel in London in March 1950. The capacity of the ballroom was taxed to its limit of 450 and in March 1951, the jubilee year of the Association, the function was held for the first time in the Great Room, where it has been held ever since with four-figure attendances. Tragically, during the intervening period, the Association suffered two sad losses. Lord Wardington, the President, died on 7 October 1950 and, a few weeks later on 27 November James Braid passed away.

It was becoming clear to those involved in the Association's finances that a major re-appraisal was needed. At the 1951 annual meeting subscriptions were raised and Charles Roe, defending the increase, alluded to the great amount of extra work undertaken by a staff of two shorthand typists and one office girl, who had to carry out all details of tournaments 'to the smallest degree'. The income of £3957 for the year included a contribution of £1474 from the Tournament Fund, being the agreed proportion of the office expenses in consideration of the work in connection with tournaments. It was clear that the revenue from subscriptions was insufficient to keep the Association solvent, and from then onwards the tournament revenue, and consequently the status of tournament players, became an increasingly important factor. The

Association was in fact entering upon a new era. What nobody envisaged was the speed and extent of the expansion and the magnitude of the changes in personnel and organization which the next twenty years were to bring.

CHAPTER SIXTEEN
The US boom begins

While the British tournament circuit was taking shape the Americans were going through a very similar stage of slow development. Although the US tour, as it is called, with tournaments played all the year round and independent of climatic restrictions, is now worth more than all the other world programmes combined, it is only in comparatively recent times that such riches have been showered on the leading players. The beginnings were so modest that even a decade after the institution of the PGA Championship there was only one other event of the same class – the Texas Open, started in 1922. The expansion really began in 1927 when the Los Angeles Open was promoted with 10 000 dollars in prizemoney – a figure which must have caused as much incredulous delight among American professionals as the advent of the *News of the World* tournament had produced among British players a quarter of a century earlier. But by 1927 a recognizable tournament programme existed in Britain.

Of course there had been many competitions for professionals in the United States before the USPGA was formed. The institution of the US Open Championship in 1896 was merely official recognition of the fact that there were enough clubs and professionals to justify a regular competition, and between then and the Great War many small events were held up and down the country. To judge from the programme of the 'Fourth Annual Professional Golf Tournament' held at the Van Cortlandt Park public links, New York, 'under the auspices of the Scottish-American Golf Club', such competitions depended a great deal on the enthusiasm of exiled Scots. The programme, found in a dilapidated condition in rubbish turned out of a house in Perth, Scotland, and shown to me by Mr P. Laidlaw of Temple, Midlothian, indicates not only the heavy Scottish flavour but also the extent to which, even in those days, golf enjoyed commercial sponsorship.

The frontispiece displays a familiar photograph of Old Tom Morris, 'the Grand Old Man of Golf', and the long list of committee members bristles with Scottish names – Craig, McClinton, Dunn, Moran, Lauder, and D. Scott Chisholm, who, in an advertisement, offered to provide a Scottish Entertainment including 'the very best vocalists, comedians, Highland pipers and dancers'. This advertisement was only one of many, twenty-nine in all, including several for golf balls, which made up the twenty-four page programme. Buried in the centre were two pages giving the conditions of the tournament and the names and starting times of no fewer than forty-two competitors. They included Stewart Maiden from Carnoustie, later to be famous as Bobby Jones's coach, and Willie Anderson from St Andrews, the reigning US Open Champion. The prizemoney totalled 430 dollars (about £150).

Competitive golf in America at that time depended greatly on such amateur efforts by immigrant Scots, and there were several reasons why many years passed before US prizemoney golf aroused general public interest. No tournament, even in the 1920s, could hope to compete with baseball as an attraction for indigent Americans, so the pioneer golf events were all held in the winter and necessarily in the south and west where weather conditions were favourable.

Considering the size of the population there were very

few full-time players and even they were attached to various clubs with duties annexed to their appointments. The American public became only slowly aware of the achievements of the best players, but when the early victories of Hagen and Jones in Britain were followed by an American victory in the Ryder Cup on American soil, people began to take notice not only of Hagen but also of Leo Diegel, Johnny Farrell, Joe Turnesa, Gene Sarazen, Al Watrous, Bill Melhorn, Jock Hutchison, Horton Smith, Jim Barnes and others who were making themselves prominent by playing exhibition matches up and down the country. All this helped to interest both public and prospective sponsors and when in 1930 journalist Bob Harlow, already active as Hagen's astute manager, took on the job of organizing tournaments for the PGA things began to hum. But Harlow, who was promoting Hagen all over America and in several countries abroad, could not give undivided attention to the new role, and in 1936 the PGA appointed a full-time tournament manager. The choice fell on Fred Corcoran, a soft-speaking, beguiling Bostonian who combined the blarney of his Irish ancestry with the traditional courtesy and reserve of a New Englander.

By that time Harlow had worked up the Tour to a programme of ten tournaments worth about 50 000 dollars which then was equivalent to about £12 000 sterling, the current value of the British programme. For the remaining pre-war years two men, Commander Roe in Britain and Fred Corcoran in the United States, worked to expand their respective circuits, but all the advantages were with Corcoran. He operated, free of all other official responsibilities, in a country so large that somewhere at any time of the year it was possible to run a tournament in favourable weather. In the summer the professionals played in New England and the middle west and when snow came to the north they migrated south and west, like birds of passage, to seek sustenance in Florida, Texas and California. In Britain, on the other hand, no sponsor wanted a tournament much earlier than the end of April or later than the end of September. The financial situation also favoured the Americans. Corcoran could interest many a tycoon in the idea of putting money into a venture which would entertain the public, earn publicity, and boost the ego of the sponsor. It was also possible to play on local pride in persuading municipalities to invest in big golf. Nearly every city had a public course – in some cases several – and in the 1930s it was easy to convince people with money to spend on publicity that golf was worth while promotionally. The message got through and Corcoran's twelve-year stint with the USPGA transformed the circuit from a modest imitation of the British programme into a list of more than thirty events worth three-quarters of a million dollars. At the same period, just after World War II, the revival of the full-scale British circuit produced no more than ten tournaments worth a tenth of the American figure. Several factors including climatic limitations and lack of big money combined to reduce the rate of expansion in Britain, and although it increased dramatically in mid-century it was continuously outpaced by the phenomenal advance of the US Tour.

In 1940, before America entered the war, the leading money winner, Ben Hogan, amassed just over 10 000 dollars. Twenty years later Arnold Palmer was consistently grossing more than ten times as much and earning on his own account as much as the whole British programme was worth. Even when, in the early seventies, the European circuit including all British and Continental events was rapidly approaching the million mark, the figure for the US Tour was eight times greater. Several factors contributed to this situation but the two players just mentioned, Hogan and Palmer, had much to do with the growth of public interest, without which such expansion would not have been possible. In 1953 Hogan, miraculously restored to fitness after a road accident which everyone thought had ended his playing career, won the Open Championship at Carnoustie in his first and only attempt. It was a *tour-de-force* which gripped the public imagination, and when some time later the Hogan story was immortalized in a full-length film 'Follow the Sun', the game entered into the consciousness of millions who previously had never given it a thought. From being an esoteric entertainment watched almost exclusively by people who played the game and therefore understood it, the big golf championship or tournament became popular with all sections of the community.

These developments were coincident with the start of the television era, and, thanks to the domestic screen, the star players were lauded by millions of fans, most of whom had only hazy ideas of technique but could thrill to the sight of men hitting booming drives, making seemingly miraculous recoveries from bunkers, and holing prodigious putts. From golf-watching to golf-playing was a logical step and the boom was 'on'. The hour had arrived for golf to take off into the stratosphere of universal sport and the hour produced the man – Arnold Palmer.

Son of a professional, Palmer distinguished himself as an amateur until late in 1954, when after having won the US Amateur Championship, he turned professional. Not even he, with all his determination and assurance, could have imagined the world fame and rich rewards which sprang from that decision. Within five years Arnold Palmer (the Arnold reduced to its affectionate diminutive Arnie) had become a household name and not only among golfers. He began by winning the Canadian Open. Two years later he won the US Masters and in 1960 won the Masters again, the US Open, and was voted US Athlete of the Year. In 1961 he won the Open Championship at Birkdale and repeated that victory at Troon in 1962.

Now famous on both sides of the Atlantic, his reputation
for eleventh-hour recoveries – his celebrated 'charge' –
appealed to galleries and TV watchers seeking excitement and suspense. Wherever he played in the United
States he had a faithful and enthusiastic following,
Arnie's Army, and a cult was born. Not only a cult but
also a way of life. American sponsors tumbled over
themselves to offer big prizemoney, seeing in golf with
star players like Palmer the means of getting reasonably
cheap publicity. Golf promotion had become commercially sound and a satisfying thing to do. It publicized
the product or the project, it enhanced the self-esteem
of the sponsor and provided a means of entertaining
clients in pleasant surroundings. When the idea of the
pro-am competition to precede the actual tournament
was born the picture was complete. To run a tournament, invite one's best customers to play alongside the
stars, attract big crowds and have one's name and
product projected on the TV screens – the temptation
was irresistible apart from making commercial common-
sense.

But the boom in the US Tour depended just as much
on the fact that many first-class players were emerging,
some from the amateur ranks, who could be depended
upon to give entertainment of the highest standard.
While Palmer was consolidating his position as No. 1
golfer of the moment a young man from South Africa,
Gary Player, and an ex-collegiate champion Jack
Nicklaus were preparing to challenge his position. The
story of American golf, indeed world golf, in the 1960s
is the story of the Big Three and how they pursued
their triangular rivalry. Later they had other challengers – America's Lee Trevino, Johnny Miller, and Tom
Weiskopf, Britain's Tony Jacklin and Peter Oosterhuis,
and others, but the electrifying upward surge of US
Tournament golf in the 1960s was due mainly to the
great public interest in the adventures of the Big Three.

Although fast becoming overshadowed by events in

America the British circuit was attracting many
players from overseas during the 1940s. Ever since
Arnaud Massy's onslaught in 1907 a few professionals
had made more or less regular visits from the Continent
and way back in 1934 Sid Brews, born at Blackheath,
London, but resident for a long time in South Africa,
finished second to Cotton at Sandwich. The real
challenge from the Commonwealth began after the war,
by which time Australia, New Zealand, South Africa
and Canada were producing home-bred golfers of
international quality. When golf clubs were founded in
what was then the British empire men from the Home
Country filled most of the professional posts. For many
years Sid Brews and his brother Jock ruled the roost in
South Africa, but in 1935, in the space of a few days, a
youngster named Arthur D'Arcy Locke, then only
seventeen, won both the Amateur and Open Championships of his country. His pet name was Bobby and
excited South African golfers saw in that prodigy a
successor to that other amateur Bobby in America, who
had proved himself best in the world in 1930. But
Bobby Locke did not long remain an amateur. He
turned professional in 1938 and after the war, in which
he served as a pilot in the SAAF, he became a regular
and very successful competitor on the British circuit as
well as making two impressive forays in the United
States. In ten crowded years he won the Open four
times and the Vardon Trophy thrice, as well as gaining
other titles in Europe and elsewhere. Almost as successful in tournaments at that time, although disappointed
in his efforts to win the Open, was a tough little
Australian, Norman von Nida, who won the Vardon
Trophy in 1947. He was also instrumental in persuading
a nineteen-year-old Melbourne amateur to turn professional in 1949 and Peter Thomson made an even greater
impact on British golf, winning the Open five times
between 1954 and 1965 as well as being runner-up
twice. Kelvin Nagle, winner of the Centenary Open in

1960, was another Australian who regularly played in Britain. But by that time the US Tour had become so richly tempting, and so many other opportunities were presenting themselves all over the world, that players like Gary Player, the New Zealand left-hander Bob Charles, and the Australians Bruce Crampton and Bruce Devlin, became globe-trotters, chasing the big prizes and the most seductive titles wherever they were contested.

CHAPTER SEVENTEEN

The ladies cash in

Until his unexpected death in 1977, aged sixty-eight, Fred Corcoran made many visits to Britain in various capacities, although that master of publicity never publicized his arrival. He seemed to materialize rather than appear. Standing in front of the clubhouse at Wentworth, Birkdale, Troon or St Andrews, looking at the scoreboard or surveying the scene, we would become aware of a grey-haired, chubby-faced man standing quietly at our side. 'Why, it's Fred,' we would exclaim and send him off on one of his explanations why he had come, what he intended to do; and, perhaps most important to us because we were likely to be involved, what he wanted others to do. For Fred's job was not to project himself but to represent people. We remember him on several particular occasions – at Wentworth in 1953 as manager of the US Ryder Cup side and there again three years later as promotional director of the Canada Cup (now World Cup) series. An earlier meeting, which involved me deeply in arranging the British end, was in 1951 when he brought over a team of women professionals to play matches and exhibitions at Wentworth and other places. And there was the time in 1954 when, without any warning, he telephoned one evening to say he was in London, staying at the Savoy, and could I come along? There he was, unpacking his bags and simultaneously asking me to assist him to find a British professional over fifty to play the American Senior Champion, Gene Sarazen, for the world title. That is how the Association of Golf Writers, who chose the challenger, became involved with Wm. Teacher & Sons Ltd, the Glasgow-based whisky firm who promoted the US Senior Championship and eventually ran for several successful years the series of Seniors' Tournaments in Britain.

Later on, as manager for the late Tony Lema and other Champions, Corcoran returned to his original role, but although all his enterprises were noteworthy he will certainly be remembered as the man responsible for showing that women professionals, properly trained and promoted could be public attractions as players. The inspiration stemmed from the prowess of The Babe, otherwise Mildred Didrikson Zaharias who, after beating records in the 1932 Olympic Games, took up golf with the same enthusiasm with which she had embraced athletics, and with the same success. At a time when women golfers relied almost entirely on rhythm to achieve results well below masculine standards, at least in the matter of length, she used her extraordinary physical power to hit the ball as far as any man. In an exhibition tour with Sarazen in 1935 she astounded everyone by mighty hitting and great powers of recovery. That tour made her a professional, but she was reinstated after the war and, in both the US Ladies' Championship of 1946 and the British Ladies' Championship of 1947, mowed down the opposition to achieve the double. Then she returned to professionalism and it was on her reputation that the idea of prizemoney tournaments for women was adopted, to develop into a circuit of some thirty events controlled by the Ladies' Professional Golf Association, formed in 1950. A modest programme in terms of prizemoney when compared with the men's tour, it is big enough, with all the fringe benefits accruing to successful players, to make professional golf for women in America an attractive proposition for the ambitious. But in Britain there is nothing

on which ambition can feed, for the scope for a woman
professional is limited virtually to the life of a club
professional with shop-keeping and teaching responsibilities. When in the 1930s Poppy Wingate became
assistant to her brother Syd at Templenewsam, Leeds,
and Meg Farquhar took a similar job at Moray in
Scotland they made news in golf circles, but there was
no suggestion that they might ever establish themselves
as players, even if they had the desire.

In earlier days there must have been many women
who helped their menfolk in the workshop, doing the
small finishing jobs which take up as much time as the
main ones; and Mrs Nancy Box's experience could not
have been an isolated one. She recalls her girlhood and
the activities of her father, Leonard C. Job, who laid
out the Wrotham Heath course near Sevenoaks and
was professional there till his death in 1946. Mrs Box
was employed in the clubhouse for many years and
remembers helping her father by cutting leather for
grips which she fitted to clubs with tacks and twine; as
well as pouring lead into clubheads and repainting golf
balls by rolling them in paint-covered hands. Nancy
Job, as she was then, was nevertheless an amateur and
played in the Girls' Championship at Stoke Poges in
1925. But even if she had wished to make golf her calling
there would have been no chance to do more than work
and serve in the shop.

More recently there have been several cases of women
turning professional with thoughts of earning money by
playing, and several originally took advantage of a
change in PGA rules which enabled women to become
members. They entered professional golf with varying
degrees of success, but Vivien Saunders not only took
the plunge but also swam strongly and well. A former
Curtis Cup international, she abandoned the amateur
ranks in 1969 and has done very well as coach
at golf centres. But her opportunities for earning
prizemoney have of necessity to be found mainly in

the United States, where she is a member of the Ladies' PGA.

Many more British amateurs would have to follow Miss Saunders's example before any sponsor could be persuaded to promote a tournament solely for their benefit, and the success of such an event would depend almost entirely on the presence of a representative number of American girls. When the Colgate-Palmolive tournament was instituted in 1974 at Sunningdale the Americans were the stars of the show and this was much the same with the second event in 1975. The US players created great interest by their modern dress and bearing, their sophisticated approach to the publicity value of their actions, and above all the high standard of their golf. Secure from masculine competition, they all looked formidable, and certainly impressive in comparison with their leading British rivals. The inducements to make the Atlantic crossing were not insignificant. The prizemoney totalled £30 000 and the Americans were sure of winning most of it. There were challengers from Japan, Canada, West Germany, South Africa and of course from Britain, and it was indeed a Japanese girl, Chako Higuchi, who came nearest to beating the best Americans. She finished third behind Donna Young and Sandra Palmer, Donna being five under par for a seventy-two holes total of 282 and beating her fellow-American by two strokes. The first British player, seventeen strokes behind the winner, was an amateur, Angela Bonallack, wife of Michael Bonallack, five times British Amateur Champion.

When Fred Corcoran handed over to others in the early 1960s the US women's circuit was well established and many young players were competing with enthusiasm for titles and cash. The most successful at that time was Mickey Wright, regarded as the natural successor of The Babe since she also had the power, the stamina and the determination that makes champions.

Her career in full competition lasted just over a decade, beginning in 1963, during which she won more than sixty tournaments and earned in prizemoney alone nearly 200 000 dollars. She also inspired those who followed her. Judy Rankin, who won the 1974 Colgate tournament at Sunningdale, Donna Young the 1975 winner, Kathy Whitworth, Carol Mann, Joanne Carner, who as Joanne Gunderson was five times women's amateur champion of the United States; Sandra Haynie, Sandra Post and the glamorous Laura Baugh are some of the names regularly appearing at or near the top of the list in the US tournaments. Kathy Whitworth has stolen most of the limelight and so far has won more tournaments than Mickey Wright and certainly much more cash since she in comparison with Mickey, like Nicklaus in comparison with Palmer, has profited by the phenomenal increase in prizemoney.

The American women's circuit has shown what women can do in a field so long restricted to men. Whether the rest of the world will develop in the same way is problematical, but there was a significant step in that direction when the 1976 tournament at Sunningdale was re-named Colgate European Women's LPGA Championship, and blessed with a massive increase of prizemoney from £30 000 to £50 000. The winner's prize was doubled to £10 000, the sponsors claiming this to be equal to the top prize in European events for men; and the inclusion of the initials LPGA indicated that the tournament was officially recognized by the US Ladies Professional Golfers' Association. It is not impossible that other sponsors in Britain or on the Continent will eventually contribute to a 'European Tour' and – who knows – create an incentive leading to a new breed of British women professionals.

The Professional Golfers' Association took an important step towards that end when, early in 1977, they reached an agreement with the Ladies' Golf Union for the control of women golfers embracing a professional

5

career. The agreement had the effect of giving women equal opportunities with men for attending the PGA Training School or becoming Tournament Playing members. This was considered essential in view of a proposal to establish a women's professional 'tour' in Britain.

CHAPTER EIGHTEEN
Golf worldwide

Half a century ago no country had anything which might have been described as a tournament circuit. But for many years now, in addition to the extensive American Tour and the substantial British and European promotions, sizeable programmes have developed in Australasia, Africa, Canada and the Far East, with smaller ones in other areas. This worldwide spread of prizemoney golf which now sends players of many nationalities jet-flying to all parts in search of cash and credit has been built up since World War II, and one of the pioneers was Peter Thomson, who helped to promote tournaments in Australia and New Zealand. From this beginning was born the Far East circuit worth well over a million dollars, which takes the competitors to Japan, the Philippines, Formosa and other parts of the Eastern hemisphere. Africa's tournaments, including those in South Africa and Zambia, Nigeria and other independent states, are worth more than a quarter of a million dollars, about the same as the Australian and New Zealand programmes. Canada naturally has a more modest list because most of her leading players compete on the US Tour.

These and other figures mean that sponsors all over the world are offering well over twelve million dollars, translated into pounds sterling, francs, pesetas, lire, yen and half a dozen other currencies, to attract the best players to their particular promotions. The fact that the lion's share of the bonanza goes to Americans does not dull the keenness of others, merely inspires them to greater efforts. The United States holds the winning cards because, apart from the pre-eminence of Americans in play, challenged by a select company of foreigners, the US Tour is open only to those who have passed a stringent test. Every year hundreds of hopeful Americans and a few from other countries compete in a tense, nerve-wracking contest for a pitifully small number of places, and retention of those places depends on the subsequent performances of the lucky ones. The system is harsh but the rewards for the survivors can be high.

Outside the United States it is a free-for-all because sponsorship can be obtained and retained only if a sufficient number of players of international standing can be persuaded to compete. If the persuasion sometimes takes the form of offering appearance money or equivalent bait it is a fact of tournament life, and lesser-known players have recourse only to a determination to gain the charmed circle. USPGA regulations severely restrict the extra-territorial activities of the leading players by requiring their participation in most of the major American events, and the rewards elsewhere, except in a few cases, are not large enough to encourage long absences from the US Tour. Americans go in some force to Britain for the Open Championship mainly because it is one of the four big events of the year in their eyes, the others being the US Open, US Masters and the USPGA Championship. When Bobby Jones climaxed his short but brilliant career in 1930 by winning the Open and Amateur titles of both Britain and America in the one season that was regarded as the classic grand slam. But with the modern emphasis on professional golf, and so many players of Championship class forsaking the amateur ranks, the target has become the four prizemoney contests mentioned.

For some years before and just after World War II the British Open seemed to lose favour with the Americans, but the victories of Hogan and Palmer, coupled with an adjustment of dates which allowed Americans to play in their own championship and then fly to Britain, restored it to its former prestige, assisted of course by greatly increased prizemoney. The first big boost in money was made to celebrate the centenary in 1960, and annual increments since then brought the total to £100 000 for 1977, with the winner, American Tom Watson, taking £10 000, a hundred times more than the £100 Walter Hagen received at Sandwich in 1922. Hagen is said to have given the money to his caddie and remarked that the title alone would be worth £10 000 to him back in the States.

Prizemoney, of course, is by no means the sole income of the star players – in some cases not even the main income. They can and do make a lot of cash on the side in many ways, and some become dollar millionaires in the process. In 1972 Jack Nicklaus became the first player in history to reach 300 000 dollars in annual winnings and how much he netted from other sources can only be guessed. Since his great rival Arnold Palmer was said to have made a million dollars in one year while winning 100 000 on the course the guesses can range far and wide. By 1972 Nicklaus for several years had been the man to beat. He won the Open at Muirfield in 1966, having been runner-up two years earlier, and after finishing second in 1967, 1968 and 1969, won the title once more in 1970. Two years later he finished second again – to Lee Trevino in a nerve-shattering final round at Muirfield. Known as the Golden Bear because of his bright hair and his habit of crushing the opposition, Nicklaus in 1973 achieved a world record by completing a tally of fourteen wins in recognized major title events. It had taken him fourteen years to beat the record set up by a great Bobby Jones in 1930, and although the amateur's thirteen wins were

gained in only eight years, the merit of Nicklaus's performance lay in being achieved against much greater
opposition than anything experienced by the champions
of fifty years ago.

Palmer had to dwell rather in Nicklaus's shadow
although bursting into the sunshine now and then, and
Player kept himself in the picture with his usual
determination, confounding everyone by winning the
Open in 1974 at Lytham. Other challengers for
Nicklaus included Lee Trevino, who beat him into
second place when winning the Open at Muirfield for
the second successive year. Johnny Miller and Tom
Weiskopf, who won the US Open and the British title
respectively in 1973, were other Americans who came
to the fore in the 1970s and with Hale Irwin winning
the US Open in 1974, Tom Watson the British Championship in 1975 and 1977 and Miller the same title in
1976, there seemed to be no dearth of youngsters in the
USA who were skilful enough to play the shots and
tough enough to stand the stress and strain of modern
prizemoney golf.

British golf by comparison was in the doldrums during the same period. In 1969 Jacklin became the first
home player to win the Open since 1951; and a few
months later, still holding that title, he caused a sensation by winning the US Open, the first British player to
do so for fifty-one years. Moreover, he won by seven
strokes. This was the highspot of his career and since
then he has played a less prominent role, overshadowed
by Peter Oosterhuis, who won the Vardon Trophy
three years running and in 1973 went very near to
winning the US Masters, finishing third after leading
on three rounds. In 1974 he finished second to Player
in the Open and at the age of twenty-four could look
back on six very satisfying years. Jacklin and Oosterhuis
entered professional golf in widely different ways.
Jacklin became an assistant at seventeen, just as
hundreds of fine players had done over the years.

Oosterhuis at the same age was still at Dulwich College, which he did not leave until after representing Britain in the 1967 Walker Cup match. In turning professional in 1968 with an impressive amateur record he followed the modern pattern.

Player, like Jacklin, turned professional at seventeen with no amateur reputation behind him, but became even more famous than his celebrated predecessor Bobby Locke because he went out boldly to challenge the Americans on their own ground. Locke it is true made two very successful winter trips in the United States and in one of them finished top money winner. But whereas Locke competed regularly in Britain, Player concentrated on the American Tour, with such success that in 1961 he won the US Masters and finished top money winner. When he won the Open for the third time at Lytham his total of major Championships reached eight in a professional career spanning twenty-two years.

Player, Palmer and Nicklaus, although unlike in style and method, have one thing in common – an aggressive attacking approach to the game. The will to win is evident in all they do and they are mainly responsible for the rise of many young players who observed that determination and application, hard work, tough thinking, and muscular activity to the very limit of physical capacity, brought rich rewards, whereas a classic style was useless without mental and physical capacity. The upsurge of newcomers able to read and understand the message was not confined to the western world. Peter Thomson was not built in the Player-Palmer-Nicklaus mould – he won the Open five times by sheer consistent accuracy and in a stylish way – but the Australians who followed him had absorbed the new ideas, particularly Bruce Devlin and Bruce Crampton, who concentrated with profit on the US Tour, and later Jack Newton, the disconsolate loser in the cliffhanger duel with Tom Watson at Carnoustie.

The message also penetrated to the Far East. In 1957 Japan won the World Cup in Tokyo and one of their players, T. Nakamura, took the individual title. In 1972 the World Cup was won by Taiwan (Formosa) with Japan finishing second above South Africa and the United States. One of the Formosan players, Lu Hiang Huan, had achieved international prominence in the previous year when he was known as 'Mr Lu' to thousands of spectators who saw him doffing his pork-pie hat above a ready smile as he fought Trevino to the last putt at Birkdale.

All over the world golfers with grit and skill are contesting the big prizes, helped by jet travel and the apparent willingness of sponsors to donate large amounts of money to attract the best players. While the US Tour remains almost a closed shop anything like a worldwide programme with a central organization is out of the question. Indeed some pessimists fear that if the peak has not been reached it isn't far away and that a fall, steep or gradual according to circumstances, lies on the other side. In half a century prize-money golf has grown from a few seeds to an abundant harvest. Are there lean years to come? No one knows. But one thing is certain. The tournament explosion has created an enormous population of golfers supplied mainly by club professionals selling the equipment produced by large firms backed by efficient sales organizations and massive advertising programmes. Tournaments may become fewer in number. Sponsors may drop out without being replaced. Big firms might find other outlets for their publicity expenditure or governments make changes in policy. But the future of golf itself and therefore of the club professional is assured, and the PGA, the USPGA, and similar Associations in other countries, will remain in good heart. They were founded on more substantial foundations than the shifting of the tournament scene.

TOP: *Cheering them home. The stampede to the home green as the 1957 Ryder Cup match drew to a close at Lindrick.* H. W. Neale

The moment of triumph. Dai Rees with the Ryder Cup chaired by his team at Lindrick in 1957. Bernard Hunt, Ken Bousfield, Eric Brown and Harry Bradshaw to the fore. H. W. Neale

LEFT : *Top of the world. Tony Jacklin with the Open Championship Cup at Lytham in 1969.* H. W. Neale

BELOW : *'The Commander' with friends. Charles Roe, flanked by George Gibson, then Managing Director of the Professional Golfers' Co-operative Association, and Lord Brabazon of Tara, then President of the PGA, at a dinner given in his honour on his retirement in 1961.* H. W. Neale

OPPOSITE : *Lord Derby, President of the PGA, lays the cornerstone of the new headquarters at The Belfry, Sutton Coldfield. Looking on are (left to right) Jack Hargreaves (Captain, 1977), Colin Snape (Secretary, PGA), Bryon Hutchinson (Captain, 1974), David Thomas, Lord Brabazon and Peter Butler (Captain, 1972). Lord Brabazon is son of the former PGA President, after whom the Brabazon course at The Belfry, designed by Thomas and Peter Alliss, is named.* PGA Collection

OPPOSITE BELOW : *An artist's impression of The Belfry, with the new PGA Headquarters on the right.* PGA Collection

Head office and regional secretariat assembled at The Belfry for the opening of the new headquarters. Standing (left to right): Colin Snape (Secretary, PGA), Jack Hargreaves (Captain, PGA), Robert Wilkinson (North Region), Brian Campbell (Irish Region), Maurice Woodbine (Midland Region), Donald Case (Southern Region), Edwin Moore (Assistant Secretary), Malcolm Mitchell (Scottish Region). Seated is Michael Harris (Western Region). PGA Collection

The Tournament Players' Division team. Marina Bray (left) and Jennifer McKenzie (centre) in the 'uniforms' they wear when assisting the directors at tournaments. The, less glamorous, males are (standing, left to right) George O'Grady (Tournament Director), Guy Hunt (TPD Committee), Tony Gray (Tournament Director), Dai Rees, C.B.E. (TPD Committee), Eddie Carter (Chief Recorder) and (seated, left to right) Ken Schofield (Secretary, TPD), John Jacobs (Consultant) and Neil Coles (Chairman, TPD). H. W. Neale

CHAPTER NINETEEN
Players far from pleased

The two decades which took golf into the 1970s were marked not only by the tournament explosions in Britain and the United States as well as in other parts of the world, but also by a tremendous growth on the business side. Sophisticated marketing and high-pressure advertising by the big manufacturers forced even the least business-minded professional to take an interest in eye-catching display and modern selling practice. In such matters Britain for a long time lagged well behind America, mainly because of the legacies of the nineteenth century, when professionals were mainly humble ill-educated folk and most golfers conservative and class-conscious. In the United States a more democratic atmosphere prevailed and the rapid growth of the game embracing all sections of the community stimulated the development of a flourishing industry using modern production and selling methods. The British professionals were perhaps slow to learn but eventually profited by the lesson, and it is unfortunate that the dramatic increase in number and value of tournaments, providing sudden fortunes for the most successful players, has tended to obscure the continuous and equally remarkable progress in less glamorous fields. Yet the benefits of keen and intelligent application to business, although perhaps lower in intrinsic value, have the advantage of being more equally shared and longer lasting.

Obviously the tournaments are so many shop-windows for professional golf, making the headlines and providing the publicity. The PGA would never have reached affluence and prestige without them. But the backroom boys must not be forgotten. Only about one-fifth of the PGA members play in tournaments, many of them irregularly, and few of the regulars make enough money to depend solely on tournament play for a rewarding career. The other four-fifths, club professionals first and foremost, are the backbone of the Association and serve club golfers from youth to retirement. They are the men who helped to develop the Professional Golfers' Co-operative Association from modest beginnings, and their support brought about the million-pound turnover in 1960 and enabled George Gibson to build even more strongly during the remaining ten years of his active connection with the Association.

By 1960 when the million-pound turnover was achieved the Association's headquarters on an upper floor in George Square, Marylebone, had become entirely inadequate, and Gibson found a splendid substitute in a building near Putney Bridge which provided plenty of space for a large show-room, several offices, and storage and dispatch facilities on the lower floor. The freehold was bought and there, during the remaining decade of his rule, Gibson was able to expand and develop ideas which had been impracticable in the confined space of George Square. During the formative years the policy of opening provincial centres progressed steadily. The first of these was started in Corporation Street, Manchester, quickly transferred to larger premises, being established after the war in Piccadilly Street. In 1936 Gibson opened a branch in Birmingham and a few years later one in Glasgow.

During his thirty years as manager and later managing director George Gibson saw tremendous changes in the business side of golf. In the 1920s most professionals considered it sufficient to stock clubs, bags, balls and other essentials and few golfers expected them to do more. But the PGCA began promoting the sale of waterproof clothing, shoes, pullovers, umbrellas and other accessories, and this policy not only increased the trading potential of the average professionals but also awakened clubs to the need for better accommodation than the wooden huts or shacks which in most cases had been thought adequate. The big advance in the PGCA turnover since World War II reflected the fact that professionals, by better display methods, improved merchandizing and more enterprising sales techniques, were enabled to compete much more efficiently than before with the sports shops and departmental stores. By 1970, when he retired, George Gibson had taken the turnover to £2 000 000 and handed over to his successor a flourishing concern ready to grow even bigger. In 1971 Marshall Lumsden arrived from British Steel Shafts (now Accles and Pollock) to be managing director, and two years later the turnover had reached £4 000 000. The roaring inflation of the period, of course, contributed to that rapid increase, but it was due also to several other factors, including improved trading methods, modernized administration and excellent progress in the export markets. Obviously internal reorganization was necessary to keep pace with the increase in business. A computer was installed to deal with accounts, stocks and other administrative matters, and large-scale reconstruction of the internal lay-out was undertaken. About ninety per cent of PGA members are shareholders of the PGCA and since this means taking up £100 in shares and a commitment to trade with the PGCA the strength comes from the rank and file.

There was a new spirit among club professionals of all degrees. Instead of complaining about competition from the big stores – as many had done in the past – they were carrying the war to the enemy by adopting similar methods of display and sale, helped by a PGA move to provide qualified advice. In 1950 a convention held after the annual general meeting discussed trade, teaching, window-dressing and other matters. The first lecturers were Mr Rodway Stephens, chartered accountant and valued PGA vice-president, on bookkeeping and income tax, and a member of the LCC Distributive Trades Council on display and window-dressing. In the same year a scheme was launched to help young golfers with film strips and other tuition, and, from the work of a committee chaired by Lord Teviot, came Golf Foundation Ltd. This non-profit-making organization was started in 1952 to provide mass tuition for school pupils. In the first year only eight schools participated, but it grew rapidly to hundreds of schools and thousands of girls and boys, thanks mainly to the voluntary help of dedicated friends of golf and the hard work of many PGA members who gave much of their time and a lot of enthusiasm. In 1976 tuition was being given to 31 000 pupils from 1473 schools.

Unfortunately, despite the obvious importance and influence of activities which increased the prosperity of professional golf and by tuition introduced large numbers of children and adults to the pleasures of the game, the interest for the general public lay in the much-publicized tournaments and the competing stars – an attraction increased tenfold when frequent television coverage brought the big events to the fireside.

Public interest in Britain received a somewhat unexpected but none the less welcome boost in 1957 when the home side won the Ryder Cup at Lindrick in Yorkshire. The last British win had been gained twenty-four years earlier, and it was perhaps natural for observers to accept this depressing state of affairs as normal, despite the near miss in 1953, when the team led by Henry Cotton at Wentworth ran the Americans so close that a missed putt on the home green in the decisive game made all the difference between defeat and a tie. When the Americans won the foursomes at Lindrick by two points it seemed that history would repeat itself, in view of their past performances in singles. But the home players went into the singles full of spirit, landing some early telling punches; and as the day wore on the pressure on the Americans grew greater and the enthusiasm of the spectators acted as a spur. It was an astonishing landslide for the visitors. They lost the singles 1½–6½ and the whole match by three points.

The scenes at the finish were memorable and no one was more delighted than Dai Rees, the Captain, whose dauntless spirit had inspired his men. For him it was the highspot, if not the culmination, of a successful career which had started in 1936 when, a fledgling of twenty-three and still an assistant, he had won the PGA match-play Championship. In the following year he made the first of nine successive playing appearances in the Ryder Cup series and won his single against Byron Nelson, the most successful US golfer of the time. Despite his impressive performances in matches and tournaments all over the world Rees never won the Open Championship, being three times runner-up, but his record pays printed tribute to one who never relaxed in his efforts on the course and was still playing well enough in his sixties to merit comparison with the grand old man of American golf, Sam Snead. They were born within a few months of each other and had comparable careers, for Snead played in seven Ryder Cup matches as well as being Captain, and like Rees, never won the Open Championship of his own country.

From the early 1960s the British circuit, despite its limited climatic scope, expanded at more or less the same rate as did the US Tour, although of course at a much lower level of values. The money poured into golf by sponsors of all kinds did much more than help the fortunate few to win big money and concentrate on competitive play to the exclusion of all other profes-

sional activities. It enhanced the prestige of the PGA
and improved the finances so much that the days of
frugality and struggle were over. But the unexpected
prosperity, because it stemmed mainly from tournament
golf, tended to widen the cleavage which had existed
for many years between the regular players and the
much larger numbers of PGA members whose interests
were mainly on the business and welfare side.

The first half-century had passed without serious
disagreement on policy and administration but in the
early 1950s many of the playing professionals adopted
contentious attitudes which aroused fears of a split.
The root cause was dissatisfaction with stagnation in
the tournament programme. The post-war jump
yielding £24 000 in 1946 had made so little progress
that the 1954 programme was worth only just over
£25 000, having totalled £30 000 in the previous year.
It seemed that some sponsors were dropping out without
being replaced. This situation, contrasting strongly
with the acceleration on the US Tour, was so critical
that in July 1954 a special general meeting, demanded
by the players, debated ways and means of improving
matters. Among the reforms suggested were better
relations between the Association and the Press, value
for money for the spectators in facilities and information, seeding draws, using walkie-talkies for course
communication, finishing tournaments on Saturdays
instead of Fridays, and increasing the differential
between the top awards and those at the bottom of the
list. There were also proposals to limit the number of
tournaments open to overseas players and allow
promising amateurs greater ease of entry into PGA
membership.

The reformers were met part of the way by a decision
to raise to twenty-five the minimum age for accepting
members, and to invite three leading players to sit with
the Executive Committee when dealing with tournament matters. But the players remained unhappy and

were riled rather than appeased by the argument that sponsors were reluctant to accept post-Open dates in July and August, and that it was virtually impossible to run tournaments in successive weeks with a staff consisting of Commander Roe and a couple of girls. At this stage the vice-presidents and the sponsors, all influential men, took a hand. At a meeting chaired by Admiral of the Fleet Sir Charles Forbes and attended by four Executive Committee members and four regular players, it was agreed that eight tournament men be added to the tournament sub-committee. The players were quick to urge the appointment of a separate tournament manager with a small retaining fee and ten per cent of the prizemoney, on similar lines to the existing arrangement in the States. But the elected members of the Committee pointed out that American competitors paid very high entrance fees, and contended that the arrangement by which the PGA charged nothing was preferable, as the whole of the prizemoney went to the players.

Events were to disprove that argument but the players had to be satisfied with moderate progress and the knowledge that they had stimulated action. The prizemoney took a distinct upward jump once the dust had settled and by 1960 had reached more than £55 000 thanks partly to a big increase in the Open total to celebrate the centenary. In the following year there were three important developments – the institution of a PGA training course for assistants; the decision, with full agreement by the players, to earmark five per cent of all prizemoney for the Tournament Fund; and the retirement of Commander Roe. The prizemoney levy yielded £2973 in the first year and increased entry fees made £3230. With other receipts the total reached about £8000 which enabled the Executive Committee to plan the appointment of a full-time successor to Charles Roe at a realistic salary.

The departure of Commander Roe was generally

regretted but regarded as inevitable in view of his age and the changed circumstances. He was in his seventy-seventh year, had given more than a third of his life to the Association, and it was no longer possible for him to deal with an expanding programme with a staff which for some time had been hard pressed. The news of his decision drew many tributes from outside and inside the Association. He was given a complimentary dinner at the Savoy, heard more kind words spoken at the subsequent PGA dinner, and was voted winner of the Golf Writers' Trophy for 1961. He had been appointed Honorary Secretary on 1 February 1934. Having then retired from the Royal Navy he could and did give full time to the work, despite his honorary standing, and for twenty-eight years, even at times during his war service from 1939 to 1945, put all his energy into making the PGA strong and financially stable as well as advancing in prestige. He was generally admired and respected and everyone took his sallies and outspoken comments in good spirit, even the 'soldiers', whom, with a twinkle in his eye, he affected to despise.

His career in the Navy began on the lowest rung, for he joined as an Enlisted Boy (2nd Class) on 30 July 1901, when only sixteen, and retired on 1 February 1930, his forty-fifth birthday, with the rank of Commander. Soon after the Great War broke out he was commissioned as Acting Mate, having passed through all the Lower Deck grades, and was serving on HMS *Hood*, the flagship of Rear-Admiral Sir Christopher Cradock, as she sailed the waters off South America. The squadron anchored in Vallenar Roads off the Chilean coast, just south of Coronel, to refuel, and Roe was landed with four signalmen to establish a look-out post on a neighbouring height. Two days later he saw *Hood* leave the anchorage, after signalling that she would be back in two or three days. She never returned, for two days later, in a running fight with superior

German forces (the Battle of Coronel) she was blown up with all hands. Roe, miraculously preserved from that holocaust, transferred to HMS *Canopus* and sailed to the Falkland Islands where he was again involved in work on shore, setting up guns and making other preparations for the defence of Port Stanley against the threatened German attack. But in the meantime the British forces had been reinforced by the arrival of another squadron, and when the Germans arrived they had a nasty surprise. In the Falkland Islands battle six enemy ships were sunk, an ample revenge for the Coronel disaster.

Soon after the battle Roe returned to Britain to spend several hard and adventurous months submarine-chasing in command of torpedo-boats in the Firth of Forth. Eventually he himself was drafted into the submarine service, and during the rest of the War and for some years afterwards commanded a succession of submarines, mainly with the Mediterranean Fleet.

After retirement he applied for, and only just failed to gain, command of the training ship *Arethusa*, despite glowing tributes to his great qualities from Admiral of the Fleet Sir Roger Keyes, Bart, and other senior officers under whom he had served. And that is how he came to put himself forward for the vacant post of Secretary of the PGA. An analysis of his career throws light on his character, ability, and temperament, and his capacity for inspiring subordinates and gaining their trust. How he would have enjoyed commanding *Arethusa* and how the boy trainees of the 1930s would have prospered under his influence! Instead, for nearly thirty years the members of the PGA had the benefit of the devoted service of one who never took on a job without putting all his heart and energy into it.

On his retirement Roe was elected an honorary life member and, by attendance at the annual meetings and many other events, maintained his interest in professional golf and gave wise advise in an unofficial

6

capacity when invited. He died on 4 March 1976, a few weeks after his ninety-first birthday, and following a mercifully brief illness. In office and in retirement he had given forty years of devoted service to the Professional Golfers' Association.

CHAPTER TWENTY
Prizemoney galore

Although the PGA owed so much to Charles Roe he was an exceptional organizer and so accustomed to the task over many years that he had absorbed almost without noticing it a gradually increasing pressure of work. It was generally realized that no successor, however able, would be able to tackle the ever-growing tournament circuit and handle the administrative work at headquarters without radical reorganization and an increase of staff. For some time a good deal of the preliminary operations at tournament venues had been carried out on a part-time basis by Eddie Carter, whose main job was to pack up the PGA scoreboard and effects at the end of one tournament and convey them to the next course on the list, where he was responsible for setting the stage and, during the event itself, posting the hole-by-hole scores communicated from the course by the walkie-talkie crews. But the Commander had to be there in person throughout the tournament, and then return to Ethelburga House to wrestle with administrative matters and prepare for the next tournament. It was just possible to handle one tournament a fortnight but the growing programme demanded almost one a week during the summer.

Thanks to the five per cent levy on prizemoney and other additions to the Tournament Fund it was possible to appoint a full-time secretary at an adequate salary and the choice fell on Lt Col T. H. Reed, who spent most of 1961 as assistant to the Commander and took over completely early in 1962. Soon afterwards Major John Bywaters was appointed assistant secretary and everything began to march. A large caravan was converted for use as the PGA travelling headquarters. Equipped with typewriters, a machine for copying scorecards and a public address system, it was towed by landrover from place to place by Eddie Carter.

An immediate sequel was an increase of prizemoney from £60 000 in 1961 to £80 000 in 1962 and the programme for the latter year included the first Senior Service tournament at Dalmahoy, near Edinburgh, where the now familiar 'tented village' made its début. A luxurious powder-room and lounge for women spectators, rooms for closed circuit TV viewing, up-to-date toilet facilities and the usual arrangements for eating and drinking were assembled under acres of canvas – a nine-days' wonder made commonplace by its subsequent adoption by all enterprising sponsors, including the Championship Committee.

The horizon was widening. More and richer tournaments were attracting larger entries and led to the introduction of the pre-qualifying system in 1963. A new and larger scoreboard replaced the PGA board and was serviced by the *Daily Express* operators who for years had been responsible for walkie-talkie communications. Eddie Carter was released for more important duties. Now working full-time he operated in the caravan office, and later, when the PGA tournament staff was extended and reorganized, he became officially tournament recorder, with duties including the preparation of Order of Merit tables and collection of monies, as well as the daily checking and printing of scorecards. He had been a familiar and popular figure at tournaments for more than a quarter of a century and his sixty-fifth birthday in 1974 made no difference. He just carried on, combining his customary efficiency with unfailing good humour.

Although the future seemed to be rosy in 1963 all was not well under the surface and when the agenda for the Annual General Meeting contained a proposal to remove tournament players from the Executive Committee it was reported that leading players had decided to break away if it succeeded. But it was rejected after a formidable contribution to the debate by Ernest Bradbeer, a former chairman, who said the tournament players had been of the greatest assistance in committee, and reminded the critics that without tournaments the continued existence of the Association would be in peril. Nevertheless praise was also due to members who, although no longer regular tournament players, made considerable contributions to the welfare of youngsters in both fields. They were the men who, inspired and led by the late Tom Jones of Maesdu, Llandudno, gave their time, experience and skills to the development of the famous PGA training courses at which assistants were instructed in all aspects of professional golf, including shop-keeping, club repairs, coaching and playing. The courses were started on a voluntary recruitment basis in 1961 and eleven assistants attended the first one at Llandudno, including Maurice Bembridge who quickly became a tournament star. What Tom Jones started others carried on, so successfully that by 1970 it was possible to establish the PGA Training Centre at Lilleshall, where all applicants for full membership of the PGA have to qualify.

When Colonel Reed retired at the end of 1965 to be succeeded by John Bywaters the British circuit was expanding at a hot pace. The 1966 programme was boosted considerably by the Carling tournament worth £71 000 and in the following year the even richer Alcan series began. But these prestigious events were meant to attract all the best players from overseas, including the United States, and they took most of the cash. This did not alter the fact that the prizemoney in

1966 totalled £180 000 and in the drive towards the quarter-million Brian Park, a Lancashire businessman who had sponsored the Ryder Cup match at Birkdale in 1965, accepted the unpaid post of executive director with responsibility for finding new sponsors, and worked hard for the next two years before retiring. Another new post, but salaried, was that of tournament administrator, a necessity because Major Bywaters, like Colonel Reed before him, found it impossible to run the administrative side at headquarters and also deal efficiently with the field work. Commander R. M. Fell, RN, was appointed and officiated at successive tournaments with the caravan as his office and Eddie Carter in the engine room. The year 1966 also saw the PGA move house for the first time since 1920. The antiquated Edwardian atmosphere of Ethelburga House, hard by the ruins of old London Wall, was exchanged for the open space of the Oval at Kennington, the famous south London cricket ground, scene of many historic matches. The breeze blowing across that celebrated stretch of turf was symbolic of the wind of change sweeping through the world of professional golf.

The appointment of Donald Case in 1968 as assistant secretary, leaving John Bywaters free for last-day appearances at tournaments and contacts with sponsors, was another necessary expansion of the staff. Soon afterwards 'Dickie' Fell resigned to take up a business post and was succeeded as field officer by Arthur Crawley-Boevey. The same year saw an important policy decision by the PGA. During the previous few years great argument had raged among amateurs and professionals alike about the relative merits of the British size ball, 1.62 inches in diameter and the larger American ball, 1.68 inches. Many influential people maintained that the supremacy of US golfers was due partly to the fact that the larger ball, being more difficult to control, demanded a high degree of skill in striking, and therefore raised the standard of play.

Others contended that whereas the 1.68 ball was suit-able for American courses it was not so for golf in Britain, particularly on seaside links where wind was often a testing factor. The dispute led an enterprising sponsor to promote a tournament in which only the big ball would be used, and the Ballantine event at Wentworth in 1961 provided an opportunity for the opposing camps to gather ammunition to support their arguments. The result was inconclusive, for although Neil Coles, with rounds of sixty-nine and sixty-five on the last day over the West Course, proved that the larger ball was manageable in skilful hands, the fact that he was five shots ahead at the finish suggested that some of his rivals had problems.

Four years later, under pressure from the big ball brigade, the PGA experimented with a rule making use of the 1.68 ball compulsory in all PGA events. Three years afterwards the rule was re-introduced for a trial period of three years which became indefinite, despite an attempt by some PGA members to revert to the smaller ball. At that time the Open Championship was not covered by the rule, the competitors having the choice of ball, but in 1975 the R and A decreed that the Open, too, would be a big-ball affair, and the triumph of the progressives was complete.

CHAPTER TWENTY-ONE
Revolt on two fronts

At this interesting stage in the development of the British circuit, events in the United States were creating an entirely new situation which was to have repercussions in Britain. In 1967, the discontent of American players over their relations with the USPGA, which catered for thousands of club professionals and only a few hundred tournament men, led to a confrontation which, without wise counsels on both sides, might have meant a complete split. Fortunately a compromise was hammered out and at the back end of 1968 the Association was reorganized to provide for a Tournament Players' Division with autonomous control over practically all major tournaments, although the Association itself remained responsible for the Ryder Cup matches and other international events, the PGA Championship and certain promotions restricted to classes.

Joseph P. Dey, Jnr, a most able and respected golf legislator, who had done a great deal to heal the rupture, was appointed Commissioner for a three-year spell, at the end of which the value of the Tour had almost doubled to eight million dollars. Joe Dey, a soft-speaking Virginian, had spent thirty-five years with the US Golf Association, retiring as Executive Director, and had a great reputation on both sides of the Atlantic, a reputation enchanced by his work for the USPGA. Over the years he had had much to do with the development and revision of the rules, and his efforts for Anglo-American golf were recognized by the R and A electing him Captain. In 1975 he 'drove into office' in time-honoured fashion at St Andrews, the second American to do so.

Joe Dey was succeeded as Commissioner by Deane Beman who carried on the good work. The continued success of the new set-up was watched enviously by tournament players in Britain and led naturally to a similar agitation for autonomy. This began in 1969 when they suggested the appointment of a 'tournament salesman' who would be occupied solely in boosting the tournament schedule in both number and value of events, to a point where Britain could in proportion challenge the successful American programme. Parity with the American circuit in financial terms was an impossible dream, for economic and climatic reasons, but it was generally felt that more progress was possible, and the idea of a tournament 'supremo' took shape.

Meanwhile the continent of Europe, which hitherto had operated at a low and erratic level, was becoming involved in an ambitious concept aimed at attracting top-class fields to the various national championships and tournaments. An important contribution to that end was made by a decision of the PGA to include the 1970 French Open, then worth £6000, among the British events counting for the Ryder Cup order of merit points. The prize list for Britain that year totalled £290 000 but this dropped to £176 000 in 1971 due to the temporary disappearance of the John Player classic and the end of the Alcan series. On the other hand all the leading Continental events had increased in value and this, together with the decision to add the German, Swiss, Spanish and Italian Championships to the Ryder Cup points list, assured promoters of the presence of all the best British and Commonwealth players.

An important step on the new road was the institution of a PGA Advisory Council of three members of the Executive Committee and several businessmen accustomed to profit-making enterprises and well known for their interest in the professional game. Early in 1971 the Executive Committee decided that the Association must go out and sell itself, and at the same time agreed that the secretariat was not equipped for that job, only because so many matters of general administration claimed constant attention. The situation demanded the appointment of an individual who would have overall control of the tournament programme, with power to negotiate directly with existing and potential sponsors, golf clubs and TV organizations. After several ideas had been discussed a satisfactory solution was found by inviting John Jacobs, a former Ryder Cup player, to be the 'supremo', and securing the services of George Simms in the fields of publicity and public relations. Jacobs had the twin advantages of being an experienced player and a keen and intelligent businessman, having in his later years been identified with a firm establishing golf centres in various parts of the country. Simms, of course, had long been established as the No. 1 specialist in golf promotion and public relations, and especially for his work as Press Officer for the Open Championship and his promoting of the Ryder Cup matches of 1965 and 1969 and other sponsored PGA events.

In a series of meetings with sponsors Jacobs obtained agreement for a minimum of £8000 in prizemoney per tournament with at least £15 000 for events held in certain special periods. His chief argument was that even one or two Ryder Cup players earned only £1000 or so on the circuit and no more than half a dozen in each tournament won enough to cover expenses. Armed with the support of the sponsors Jacobs was able to complete deals with the BBC and the ITA which ensured television coverage of eight tournaments during 1972. This meant that about half the tournaments would be screened, a proportion similar to that in the United States.

The Executive Committee's decision to appoint Jacobs and Simms was ratified by seventy-one votes to two at a meeting of players at York on 17 August 1971, and the new organization quickly got into top gear. It was estimated that the overall cost would be about £19 000 a year and early steps towards footing the bill included raising the entry fee, first to £6 per player and later to a rate of £1 for each £1000 of prizemoney. In addition any player competing in more than one tournament paid a seasonal levy of £30. It was agreed that Jacobs would be answerable only to the Advisory Council and have the tournament administration under his jurisdiction, while the PGA secretary and staff would operate as before in carrying out all the pre-tournament work.

The result exceeded most expectations. The programme for 1972, including the revitalized Continental circuit, approached half a million – double that of 1971. The half-million mark was passed easily in 1974, the third year of the Jacobs-Simms operation. By this time the minimum of £8000 for events for which top players were not necessarily available had risen to £12 000, and the figure for peak-period events from £15 000 to £20 000. Some sponsors exceeded the top total and even the younger professionals shared in the prosperity when the prize fund for the Coca-Cola under-twenty-five tournament soared from £4000 to £10 000.

Unfortunately the Association, in the midst of this surge, lost two men who had borne the heat and burden of the day for several progressive years. The resignation of Arthur Crawley-Boevey as tournament administrator in 1972 was followed by the death of John Bywaters in 1973. Crawley-Boevey, who in 1975 filled a similar post in the newly-formed organization for controlling European professional events, used to start his stint 'in the field' at 6.30 a.m. and finish about 7.30 p.m.; and he often had to travel at week-ends to be on the scene of the next tournament in time to make the necessary preparations with the help of the ubiquitous Eddie Carter. Donald Case undertook some of this preliminary spade-work, including supervision of pre-qualifying rounds, but could not easily be spared from the office. It was clear that the field-work, including pre-planning, demanded the appointment of two tournament administrators, who would virtually share duties on the basis of one going ahead to the next port of call to prepare the ground. Tony Parsonage (who resigned at the end of 1973) and Colin Snape were appointed to succeed Crawley-Boevey but within a year the death of John Bywaters necessitated another change. Colin Snape became secretary and Donald Case remained assistant secretary with his particular duties lying on the club professional side. The new organization was completed in January 1974 by the appointment of Tony Gray and George O'Grady as the new tournament administrators.

During his ten years in office John Bywaters had established a reputation for hard work, great enthusiasm, and an immense pride in the Association and its members. In particular he took a personal interest in the PGA Training Centre and the peak of his work in that direction came in 1970 with the establishment of the courses at Lilleshall, from where many young professionals have passed through the instructional classes and emerged fully qualified.

Everyone who mourned John Bywaters remembered his devotion to that cause and the John Bywaters Memorial Fund was set up to finance the Centre. His family remembered, too, and a few months after his death they added a cheque for £2000 to the £650 so far contributed by many individuals. What a wonderful way to keep alive the memory of a man who, young at heart himself, thought and worked to much for the new generation of professionals.

John Bywaters had no doubt as to the future of the PGA although with characteristic diffidence he fell short of positive assertions in public. His optimism can be gathered from this extract from a lecture he gave several times at the Assistants' Training Courses:

Where do we go from here? The future is not for me to forecast but the present facts are incontrovertible, and, I think, favourable. The Tournament Fund is in a stable condition, able to finance the new regime and also make a fair contribution to the general funds of the Association. We have more than 1500 members, a watertight training scheme, a reliable recruiting system, and the support of a growing population of golfers who are persuaded, by greatly improved salesmanship, to support the professional in his shop. The PGA is flourishing, the golf trade has been and is being most helpful, the game itself is booming, and altogether I must confess to a strong feeling of optimism.

John Bywaters did not live to see the full fruits of his labours but the PGA owes much to him, as indeed to Commander Roe and, going still further back, to those sturdy pioneers, led by John Henry Taylor, who first persuaded British professionals to organize themselves.

CHAPTER TWENTY-TWO
Towards a new horizon

Many steps had been taken to meet the players' wishes but they would not be satisfied with anything less than autonomy in their field. They wanted a Tournament Players' Division similar to that in the United States, and the annual meeting in November 1974 voted almost unanimously in favour. Unfortunately the subsequent discussions on ways and means, procedural details and the proposed changes in the constitution revealed differences of opinion which led to unforeseen and exasperating delays, as well as a good deal of Press comment on the possibility of a split. In May 1975 the players put forward their proposals for a new constitution and the Executive Committee made counter-proposals. July was a month of crisis with the players clearly determined to be independent and the Executive equally determined to preserve a measure of PGA control.

The whole matter came to a head at York on 12 August when more than a hundred players and several members of the Executive Committee hammered out an agreement in five hours of debate. Concessions were made on both sides but when the new constitution was passed at a special general meeting in November it was seen to give the players perhaps not all they had demanded, but certainly as much as they could have expected. Both sides had reason for satisfaction – the players because they were to be masters in their own house; and the Executive Committee because the Association, by the institution of a Board of Management with an independent chairman, would retain overall surveillance of PGA activities and strict control over finances. The most important outcome, from the general point of view, was that both sides by giving and taking had averted a complete rupture with unpredictable and certainly damaging consequences. So, at the beginning of 1976, the seventy-fifth anniversary year, the Association was set on a new course with two crews speeded on by a general hope that the voyage would be harmonious. The crisis, similar to that in the USPGA seven years earlier, had been settled in the same way, by common sense and compromise.

The new constitution of the PGA established a General Division as well as a Tournament Players' Division, each with three representatives sitting on a Board of Management with an independent chairman. Michael Bonallack, the greatest British amateur of his time, accepted an invitation to be first chairman, and the original members of the Board were Neil Coles, Peter Butler and Dai Rees for the TPD and Bryon Hutchinson, Douglas Smith and Jack Hargreaves for the GD. The Board is responsible for overall direction of the Association's activities and policy, with control in all vital matters including finance, assets and discipline, as well as organization of the Ryder Cup matches and the selection of official teams. Most of those special functions are carried out by the General Committee, composed mainly of two representatives each from the various geographical regions. The Tournament Players Division has overall supervision of and responsibility for all professional tournaments in the United Kingdom and Ireland with the exception of certain class or localized events such as the Seniors' Championship. TPD policy, finance and administration are controlled by committee of ten, while the operational side is handled by John Jacobs, the Tournament Administrators Tony Gray and George O'Grady, and the Tournament Secretary Ken Schofield.

No part of the Association's work is beyond the control of the Board of Management, which can discuss and decide on any matter connected with tournaments or general administration which is considered to affect the PGA as a whole. In all the preliminary negotiations there was never a suggestion that the TPD would not act with care and fidelity. But in the last resort the Board of Management, through the casting vote of the chairman in the case of a 3–3 split, can ensure that no step inimical to the welfare or interests of the Association will be taken.

The contentions of 1975 did not hamper Jacobs and his team in the search for an even richer programme for 1976, and thanks to their hard and enthusiastic work the magic million pound mark ceased to be an impossible target. The prizemoney in British events alone went up by more than £200 000 and the 1976 total for the whole of Europe, including such exclusive events as the Piccadilly World Match-play Championship at Wentworth and the Lancôme Trophy tournament in France, reached £906 500.

The million mark was duly reached and passed in 1977, and the considerable contribution made by the Continental promoters led to an interesting development – the establishment of the European Tournament Players' Division. Thirty championships and tournaments arranged for Europe in 1977 included eleven on the Continent which were worth one-third of the total prizemoney. So there was a logical reason for the move, which produced a Division controlled by a ten-man policy committee comprising six members of the British TPD and four representatives of the Continental Tournament Players' Association. The latter included M. Ballesteros and A. Gallardo of Spain, G. Mueller of Sweden and P. Toussaint of Belgium.

As 1977 dawned and the good ship PGA ploughed her twin furrows through strange waters a fresh port was visible on the horizon – new national headquarters. Arrangements were in hand for the occupation of offices at the Belfry Hotel, Sutton Coldfield, Warwickshire. The PGA were about to possess a permanent home with two championship-type courses.

CHAPTER TWENTY-THREE

A dream fulfilled

The move to the Midlands originated in 1974 when the PGA considered ways and means of transferring headquarters from Kennington Oval in London, where the offices rented in the Surrey CCC pavilion had become totally inadequate. At that juncture Ellerman Lines Ltd joined with northern brewers Greenall Whitley & Co, Ltd in a project to rebuild, extend and modernize the old Belfry Hotel at Sutton Coldfield and convert it into a residential, social and sporting centre, at an initial cost of £3 500,000 and a prospective total expenditure of about £6 000,000. As part of the development plan the consortium offered space in the new Belfry Hotel and presented the PGA with a perfect solution to the problem.

So, on 1 January 1977, the Association took over a ninety-nine-year lease of some 6000 square feet of office space rent-free – an arrangement which, in addition to providing new and spacious headquarters at no cost to the PGA made possible retention of the Oval offices for use by the Tournament Players' Division, which had to remain in London; and by secretarial personnel concerned with administrative matters conveniently dealt with in London. Another attractive feature was the establishment at Sutton Coldfield of two full-length golf courses, one of prime championship standard. The courses were designed by Peter Alliss and David Thomas. Later a former PGA Captain, Hugh Lewis, was appointed professional at the new centre.

The set-up could not have been better tailored for PGA requirements. In addition to enjoying the geographical advantage of being more readily accessible for a greater number of members, the Association had the use of two fine modern courses for tournaments, and plans were soon made to stage the Ryder Cup matches there in 1981 and 1989.

Nothing was spared to make the courses and their surroundings suitable in every way for the most ambitious promotion, with permanent installation of facilities essential for great occasions – vantage points for spectators, sites for stands, a driving range and practice areas, built-in connections for TV coverage, an undercourse telephone system, and plenty of space for the ubiquitous 'tented village'.

My personal connection with the Association goes back to the establishment of the first offices in Bishopsgate in 1921, so I was suitably impressed, indeed astonished, by the comparison between the new suite in The Belfry and the three small offices in the shadow of old London Wall, the largest of which was a 'committee room' of some 200 square feet. The most striking feature of the new headquarters was the main suite of about 1800 square feet in a podium perched on the roof of the hotel and commanding magnificent views over both courses. One could envisage the whole machinery of a major event being operated and controlled from this PGA eyrie.

The move was in fact the realization of a dream which more than one pioneer had had many decades in the past, and was in keeping with the phenomenal growth in numerical strength and international prestige of, a body which includes among its 3000 members 600 overseas professionals and 300 home-based full-time tournament players. Such figures, although indicating strong support for the tournament side, which is the shop-window of professional golf, also emphasize the fact that the PGA is fundamentally a fraternity of club professionals, with responsibility for the welfare of all members, the protection of their business interests and the training of assistants to become professionals in their turn.

To further those business interests the PGA decided to become concerned much more than hitherto in the marketing of golf products exclusive to the Association, and to that end negotiated a deal with the well-known Scottish manufacturers, Ben Sayers Ltd of North Berwick, for the production of a range of equipment, including the 'PGA Conquest' club. A logical outcome of this development, in the view of PGA officials, would have been some kind of merger or working arrangement with the Professional Golfer's Co-operative Association (see Chapters 13 and 15). Logical, because PGA members concerned with the government of the Association are, like all other members, shareholders of the PGCA. For various reasons no arrangement was possible at the outset but there seemed to be no reason why both organizations should not form one coherent whole – a PGA trading body operating for the benefit of everyone concerned.

In addition to the benefits of the rent-free suite at The Belfry the PGA obtained the sponsorship of Accles and Pollock, the steel shaft manufacturers, for the move from London, to the extent of £50 000, and the same firm also sponsored for a similar sum the Association's training school.

So, on 1 April 1977, with Secretary Colin Snape installed at The Belfry, a new chapter in the history of the PGA was opened. With the establishment of the two-tier organization the secretariat of the General Division will have little or nothing to do with tournaments, and that is all to the good because the ordinary administrative work is becoming daily more demanding as the membership grows and new ideas are developed. There was a definite need for some decentralization, and for a long time it had been felt that the long-standing establishment of eight district sections each with a club professional as honorary secretary, and which dated from the earliest years, had become out-dated and counter-productive. It was obviously unfair in the 1970s to expect a busy professional to undertake onerous duties on a voluntary basis. For this reason the members at the 1976 annual general meeting agreed to a re-grouping of the eight sections into six regions, one each for Scotland and Ireland and four for England and Wales, based on the local government boundaries introduced in 1974. This restructuring, together with the appointment of full-time salaried secretaries for the six regions, was part of the PGA policy of providing a better service for club professionals and securing greater recognition for them. Regional secretaries have the task of advising members, running information services and conducting promotional campaigns. In particular they have the job of co-ordinating local tournaments into regional circuits, so increasing the importance of events and attracting more sponsors and higher prizemoney.

Although the regional committees will manage local finance and activities, all regions will be controlled by the PGA General Committee consisting of two representatives from each region. This development was the culminating point of three years of reconstruction, and it was with a sense of having put their house in order that the officials and members welcomed the move to The Belfry. It was generally realized and conceded that great changes had come about without impairing the integrity or the philosophy of the Association and the members.

The strength of the PGA is that high standards have been set from the start and maintained, even in a changing world. The code of ethics lays down that the title must remain a hallmark of service, honesty, fair dealing and courtesy. So the aspiring assistant, in addition to passing tests of ability at the training school before qualifying as a full member, must also satisfy his elders as to his adherence to the principles of the calling. This is of great importance for hundreds of thousands of golfers who rely on professionals at private clubs and public courses for tuition, guidance in choosing equipment, and service in repairs. Yet, paradoxically, far too many golfers have far too little thought for the club professional, as they yield to the excitement of watching and reading about the stars in the big tournaments.

The cavaliers of the links who perform apparently miraculous feats in front of the television cameras and whose activities are followed by millions of people on screen and on course are far outnumbered by the many club professionals who, however much appreciated by their members, go practically unnoticed beyond the boundaries of their home courses. That distinction, now so clear, is of comparatively modern origin. Seventy years ago the average professional was regarded purely as the servant of the club to which he was attached, and made only rare competitive appearances in public. Not even Vardon, Taylor and Braid in their heyday, nor their American contemporaries, could afford to neglect their shops and members – their only source of regular income. Championships and tournaments, although making them prominent and therefore enhancing their business value, were merely the icing on the plain cake of everyday chores.

The twentieth century was well advanced before the situation changed noticeably, and not until after World War II did hundred-per-cent tournament players emerge in sufficient numbers to become a significant class. They were able to do so because of the increased interest of commercial sponsors in the publicity value of golf promotion; and this stirred the ambitions of young

amateurs who, tempted by the prospect of fame and
fortune, joined in the scramble for big prizes and
prestigious titles. In most cases the dream turned into
cruel reality as the bright-eyed hopefuls became
disillusioned. Some gained enough money each year to
cover their expenses and keep them in the race. They
were the lucky ones. The great majority pegged away
below the break-even line until they gave up the
struggle and took safe jobs as club professionals or
applied for reinstatement as amateurs.

For those good enough in play and tough enough in
temperament to keep regularly in the big money the
future looks bright. Despite gloomy forecasts heard
from time to time on the 'It can't last' theme the boom
in tournament golf goes on all over the world. A golf
tournament televised is a most valuable vehicle for
publicity. Even without television it can draw large
crowds, and an astute sponsor can profit in many ways
from the scene and the action. The spread of prizemoney golf has increased the scope for star players, and
naturally increased their numbers.

But tournaments are not fundamental to golf,
merely a by-product. Basically golf is a game which
anyone of any age or sex can play, even as a loner, with
equipment ranging from the ultra-modest to the
ostentatious. In the last hundred years it has grown
into a worldwide pastime giving enjoyment to millions
of club members, and providing a livelihood for
thousands of professionals and workers in the flourishing
industries which supply the equipment. It also provides
entertainment for millions who watch tournaments and
rich rewards for a minority of those who entertain. The
two branches of professional golf are apparently
distinct but really interdependent. The club professional
serves the amateur who supports the industry. The
player helps to publicize golf and popularize the
equipment sold by the club professionals. It is a
co-operative world and everyone depends on everyone

else. The PGAs of Britain and America now both have Tournament Players' Divisions autonomous in many ways but still part of their parent bodies. These, like the PGAs of many other countries, were founded to serve the club professional, preserve his status and foster his welfare. Those objects remain.

The lords of the links strut the fairways confidently, proudly and purposefully. They bask in the limelight and take the big cheques – but only sometimes and for a period limited by age and competitive pressures. Behind them, in thousands of smart shops stocked with all the latest in golfware, work the club professionals who form the backbone of the game. When the first PGA was founded at the turn of the century – the first professional body of that kind in the world – one of the objects was to hold tournaments 'periodically for the benefit of the younger members', and the first of those was for prizes totalling £15. Today dozens of tournaments all over the world under the auspices of many PGAs are worth together something like £10 000 000. We have come a long way from 1901 and are still more remote from those early Victorian years when men like Allan Robertson and Tom Morris touched their caps to their betters and were prepared to undertake any job on the links from caddying to playing. Their humble footsteps began the march of professional golf to its present lordly eminence in the sporting world.

Index